The Development in International Law of Articles 23 and 24 of the Universal Declaration of Human Rights: The Labor Rights Articles

The Universal Declaration of Human Rights

Series Editor

Professor Hurst Hannum

Human rights law has developed from the modest "common standard of achievement for all peoples and all nations," proclaimed by the Universal Declaration of Human Rights in 1948, to a complex and rich substantive tapestry of international and national law. The provisions of the Universal Declaration have been codified and interpreted by a growing number of international bodies, most significantly by the committees created to oversee the International Covenant on Civil and Political Rights and the International Covenant on Economic, Social and Cultural Rights, each of which has over 140 state parties. In addition, the Declaration has served as a model for national constitutions and statutes, many specifically designed to reflect the Declaration's provisions.

Inspired by the fiftieth anniversary of the Declaration, the Universal Declaration of Human Rights Series analyzes the development of the Declaration's norms and their status in contemporary international law. The Series consists of approximately 20 volumes, each dealing with a substantive right (or group of rights) set forth in the Universal Declaration of Human Rights. Each volume is authored by an expert in human rights generally and in the particular subject addressed. Each book provides a comprehensive, legally-oriented analysis of the rights concerned, understood within the political context in which implementation of human rights must occur. The issues addressed include an examination of the legislative history of each right at the time of its adoption, the right's subsequent articulation and interpretation by international bodies and in subsequent international instruments, and, where feasible, a survey of state practice in defining and enforcing the right. When completed, the Series will constitute an encyclopaedic guide to the content of universally recognized human rights in the twenty-first century.

VOLUME 5

The titles published in this series are listed at *brill.com/udhr*

The Development in International Law of Articles 23 and 24 of the Universal Declaration of Human Rights: The Labor Rights Articles

By

Lee Swepston

BRILL
NIJHOFF

LEIDEN | BOSTON

Library of Congress Cataloging-in-Publication Data

Swepston, Lee, author.
The development in international law of Articles 23 and 24 of the Universal Declaration of Human Rights : the labor rights articles / by Lee Swepston.
pages cm. — (The Universal Declaration of Human Rights ; volume 5)
Includes bibliographical references.
ISBN 978-90-04-24454-2 (hardback : alk. paper) — ISBN 978-90-04-24455-9 (e-book) 1. Labor laws and legislation, International. 2. United Nations. General Assembly. Universal Declaration of Human Rights. I. Title.

K1705.S925 2014
344.01'01—dc23

2014007716

This publication has been typeset in the multilingual 'Brill' typeface. With over 5,100 characters covering Latin, IPA, Greek, and Cyrillic, this typeface is especially suitable for use in the humanities. For more information, please see brill.com/brill-typeface.

ISBN 978 90 04 24454 2 (hardback)
ISBN 978 90 04 24455 9 (e-book)

This book is printed on acid-free paper.

Contents

Contents

The Text of Articles 23 and 24

Articles 23 and 24 of the Universal Declaration of Human Rights
Rights at Work

Article 23

(1) Everyone has the right to work, to free choice of employment, to just and favourable conditions of work and to protection against unemployment.
(2) Everyone, without any discrimination, has the right to equal pay for equal work.
(3) Everyone who works has the right to just and favourable remuneration ensuring for himself and his family an existence worthy of human dignity, and supplemented, if necessary, by other means of social protection.
(4) Everyone has the right to form and to join trade unions for the protection of his interests.

Article 24

Everyone has the right to rest and leisure, including reasonable limitation of working hours and periodic holidays with pay.

 | DOI 10.1163/9789004244559_002

Introduction

The human rights enunciated in these two articles of the UDHR concern aspects of rights related to work. This part of international human rights law is often neglected in human rights textbooks and teaching, and indeed is often omitted from the work done by national human rights institutes and by non-governmental organizations concerned with human rights, as though it were a separate discipline that did not fall properly into the human rights field. This is a commonly held, but erroneous, misconception based on three factors,

The first is the politically-driven division of human rights into civil and political rights (CP) on the one hand, and economic, social and cultural rights (ESC) on the other. This was founded in the ideological conflicts of the Cold War, and consolidated by the adoption of the two major—but separate—human rights Covenants in 1966. There were superficially credible reasons for the distinctions drawn between these so-called categories of rights, based in the emphasis given to one or other set by the 'East' and 'West' because each side privileged one category of rights over the other. The 'West' took the position that economic, social and cultural rights would flow from political freedoms, while the 'East'—unwilling to accord civil and political liberties to their citizens—took the position that it was most important to ensure economic stability and wellbeing before venturing into the dangerous waters of democracy.

The second, though related, reason is based in the Western notion of individual rights being the only ones that can properly be called human rights. Collective rights—which are characteristic of many ESC rights—cannot in this view properly be called human rights. This is still today the more or less official position of the United States, the United Kingdom and a few others in international discussions. Another aspect of this same question is the notion that ESC rights could not be achieved without economic development, while CP rights are accessible for every nation without financial cost—another flawed assumption, discussed in more detail below.

Finally, there is the more prosaic reason that United Nations human rights bodies (except the Committee on Economic, Social and Cultural Rights) have traditionally focused on civil and political rights, in part because of the existence of the International Labor Organization (ILO) and other organizations, such as the United Nations Educational, Scientific and Cultural Organization (UNESCO), whose mandates cover many of the ESC rights; combined with the long abstention of the ILO from asserting itself as a human rights organization

 | DOI 10.1163/9789004244559_003

and from taking an active part in the UN Commission on Human Rights (later the Human Rights Council) and related bodies.

There is also an under-analyzed factor, which is that national representation in the parts of the UN system dealing with human rights has normally been assured by ministries of foreign affairs, and not by national ministries that actually deal with economic, social and cultural rights. Foreign ministries have a tendency to act in a defensive posture to ensure that they are not branded as violating human rights, as well as the political imperative of maintaining good relations with other States.

The first three of these factors began to fade away with the end of the Cold War. One major contributing factor to the reunification of human rights as an integrated discipline was the series of major conferences convened by the UN in the 1990s, with for our purposes the World Conference on Human Rights held in Vienna in 1993 being the main precipitating event. The World Conference affirmed[1] that:

> 5. *All human rights are universal, indivisible and interdependent and interrelated. The international community must treat human rights globally in a fair and equal manner, on the same footing, and with the same emphasis.*

This was a major contribution to the equal treatment of ESC rights, which has progressed steadily since then. Nevertheless, both national and international human rights bodies tend, in general, to regard economic, social and cultural rights as less important, less urgent and less newsworthy that civil and political rights.

A Note on the Impact of International Standards and Supervision

The standards adopted at the international level have an impact at the national level, but that impact varies by kind of standard, the quality of supervision, and national circumstances. So, while a global evaluation of impact is hard to make, the factors governing the kind of impact can be spelled out.

Economic, social and cultural rights are sometimes thought to demand more expensive and difficult implementation measures than do civil and political rights, and therefore are said to be less simple to implement. This is too

1 *Vienna Declaration and Programme of Action*, adopted by the World Conference on Human Rights in Vienna on 25 June 1993, paragraph 5.

great a generalization, as there are many different kinds of standards in both of these general groupings. In the case of standards affecting the workplace, however, there are also very real economic benefits resulting from implementation. Put at the simplest level, injured workers are not productive and someone must pay for their maintenance and rehabilitation, whether this is paid from family resources, by the employer or from the public purse. Implementation of the right to a safe and healthy working environment can involve costs, but these are more than repaid in efficiency and in not losing productivity. Discrimination in the workplace excludes or undervalues the contributions of women, minorities and others, resulting in net losses to personal income and national economies. Forced labor and child labor are inefficient in themselves, and carry long-term social costs. In short, the standards examined here are those globally agreed to be necessary both to human dignity as well as to a healthy economy, and there is therefore an inherent incentive to implement them.

Whether or not that incentive is recognized is, of course, another matter. It is regrettable that this obvious relationship between rights and development is not always sought after or achieved. Nevertheless, implementing these standards as quickly as possible will result in net gains in human welfare and in national economies. Why then, is there such an implementation gap?

When governments ratify international conventions they obligate themselves in international law to observe their requirements. Different international organizations have established different ways of examining how these obligations are carried out, and pointing out deficiencies to the governments concerned. The impact of these supervisory measures varies, depending on the subject, the method of supervision, and the kind of rights being examined, as well as on the stage of national economic and social development at which such observations are made.

International organizations have been given little enforcement power, with the exception of the European and Inter-American human rights courts. For the most part international supervisory mechanisms rely on a 'name and shame' approach, with no direct enforcement available. Whether this works—and consequently whether the standards described here are given effect—depends on several factors.

Some States appear to ratify international human rights treaties as an exercise in public relations directed either towards their own people or towards the outside, with no intention to take effective steps to implement them. In other cases ratification expresses a long-term aspiration, and the State is aware that it has little likelihood of implementing them immediately but does intend to do so at some future time. Sometimes States ratify them as an incentive, and are willing to bear the international criticism while moving towards implementation. In most cases international supervisory mechanisms will take the difficulty of implementation into account, as long as efforts are being made.

In most cases of violations, however, there is an intention to apply these treaties but there are factors preventing States from fulfilling their intention.

Most violations arise from insufficient resources, on either the intellectual or financial levels, or from a lack of effective governance. This does not excuse non-compliance, though it may help to explain it. A large number of developing countries in particular have few government officials capable of drafting effective legislation or regulations, or of putting effective law enforcement (including labor inspection) into place. This kind of situation may be an unrecognized problem at the time of ratification, or it may arise after ratification, for instance when there is a loss of government revenue and administrative capacity in a recession, or in States going through social upheaval.

There are also cases in which standards such as those on freedom of association or non-discrimination are ratified but conflict with the national political or social systems. In these cases international obligations or supervision will have little immediate effect, but in the best of cases will serve as guidance and inspiration when the political situation changes. Examples are readily available, such as the implementation of ratified international conventions in countries of the former USSR once they acquired independence, especially with regard to freedom of association (the *Solidarity* phenomenon in Poland, for example). In South Africa, account began to be taken of both freedom of association and non-discrimination instruments only after the end of apartheid, but these were then brought rapidly into the national legal framework.

Developments in Myanmar with regard to forced labor and freedom of association are another positive example. The ILO had been criticising the country for more than 30 years under the Forced Labor Convention, 1930 (No. 29), for the extensive use of forced labor as a development tool. Myanmar was equally subject to criticism in the United Nations human rights mechanisms for violations of political freedoms. Finally, a formal complaint was filed under article 26 of the ILO Constitution. A Commission of Inquiry appointed by the Governing Body delivered its report in March 1997, detailing widespread violations.[2] A resolution on the widespread use of forced labor in Myanmar was adopted by the International Labor Conference at its 87th Session

2 As will be seen below, all ILO supervisory material is available on line, especially in the international labor standards database NORMLEX. The reports of Commissions of Inquiry can be found at http://www.ilo.org/dyn/normlex/en/f?p=NORMLEXPUB:50011:0::NO::P50011_ARTICLE_NO:26 (consulted 19 November 2013).

(June 1999), and at its 88th Session (May–June 2000) the Conference adopted a resolution under article 33 of the ILO Constitution, imposing restrictions on ILO contacts with the country until the situation changed. Persistent pressure on the Government to accept help to abolish forced labor did result in the establishment of an ILO technical office in Myanmar on this subject, and slow progress was made on an entirely technical basis. But once the government changed, contacts accelerated, and in June 2013—following an address to the Conference by Mme Aung San Suu Kyi in 2012—the International Labor Conference was able to confirm that Myanmar was taking positive measures to abolish the use of forced labor and it began to lift ILO restrictions on the country's participation in the ILO.

In other words, a long-term view is often necessary, but persistent supervision, where possible supplemented by assistance, by international organizations can yield results after years of apparently futile comments.

But there are also ample negative examples, in which States persist in conduct that they know is incompatible with international human rights law. Restrictions on the human rights of women are provided for explicitly in some countries because recognizing these rights would conflict with religious law that these countries consider to be of a higher order—and in other countries they lurk in corners of the national legal regime that make it difficult for women to exercise equal economic power with men. Fragile and fearful governments do not allow trade unions to organize or work without restrictions, because they may challenge government power in a way that no other national institution can. Discrimination against certain ethnic groups, may persist in the face of widespread condemnation from outside because a high proportion of the national population believes that they are inferior. The human rights of migrant workers may be violated systematically because governments are afraid to take the hard decisions necessary to allow them to work and reside in the country without discrimination. Is international supervision and criticism futile in such cases? No. Experience shows that it is simply slower than direct measures at the national level to correct these abuses. There are times when human rights advocates must hold to the work for decades—and wait for the national system to become open to change. If you have a short attention span, then find another line of work.

CHAPTER 1

Institutional Development of International Labor Law—An Overview of Institutions and Instruments

A The International Labor Organization

There are aspects of labor-related rights in all the major human rights instruments and systems. While the International Labor Organization (ILO) is the primary body in this field, labor-related rights are also dealt with by the United Nations, the major regional organizations such as the Organization of American States and the European Union, and the development banks (the World Bank and its regional counterparts). There are also provisions on labor rights in all the major international instruments, or they have been read to cover labor-related questions.

This volume will spend most attention on the ILO, which is the premiere organization in this field, both chronologically and substantively. However, one of the main lessons to be learned in this field of study is that a thorough and complete picture of human rights cannot be drawn without considering labor-related rights as an aspect of the broader human rights canon, so the rest of the international system will also be brought in.

The ILO is the intergovernmental organization with principal responsibility for the questions covered by Articles 23 and 24 of the Universal Declaration of Human Rights. If its character as a human rights organization is only recently being recognized by human rights activists,[3] this is perhaps because it has usually avoided a "human rights" rhetoric in its long history. Since its establishment in 1919 together with the short-lived League of Nations, it has usually taken a more technical approach to rights in the workplace, and has preferred to express its aim as the pursuit of social justice rather than the promotion of human rights. Moreover, its conventions tend to be focused more on the responsibility of States than on the rights of individuals, though there are

3 See, e.g., Bartolomei, von Potobsky and Swepston, *The International Labor Organization: The International Standards System and Basic Human Rights* (Westview Press, 1996); and *Human Rights, Labor Rights and International Trade*, Compa and Diamond ed. (University of Pennsylvania Press, 1996). These were forerunners of the much longer bibliography that exists today.

 | DOI 10.1163/9789004244559_004

exceptions. However, events since the end of the Cold War in the early 1990s have forced it "out of the closet", so to speak, into becoming a more assertive party to human rights deliberations at the national and international levels, and to take more of a rights-based approach to the world of work.

1 *History of the ILO*[4]

As the industrial revolution took hold, so did public awareness of harsh working conditions and of the need for their regulation. With time, as this social regulation evolved, industrialists and trade unions became concerned that exploitation of workers in other countries could undermine the profitability of international trade on the one hand, and the growth of the concept of workers' rights on the other.

The first concerted action across borders took place in 1855 in Switzerland, when two cantons met to conclude an inter-cantonal agreement on night work and working hours. Germany convened the first international conference, in Berlin in 1890, where international labor legislation was first explored in an official forum. These efforts continued until the International Association for the Legal Protection of Workers was created in 1900, and an International Labor Office created as its secretariat, with its office in Basel, Switzerland. The first two international conferences of the Association, held in 1905 and 1906, adopted the first two international labor conventions (on the prohibition of white phosphorous in the making of matches, and on night work for women).

Efforts to convene another conference were thwarted by the outbreak of World War I. During the War, trade union organizations from both sides of the conflict agreed that a mechanism for international labor legislation should be created as part of the peace settlement. It is also relevant that all the parties understood that this first 'industrial war' had depended on the willingness of workers' organizations to defer their own ambitions for better working conditions, in the interests of national defence. These influences led to the inclusion of workers' representatives in the Peace Conference, and to proposals by a number of governments, especially Great Britain and France, for international labor questions to be included in the Conference. The establishment of the International Labor Organization was thus included in the Peace Treaty concluded in 1919, and its first Constitution was Part XIII of the Treaty of Versailles.

---

4 For a more complete history of the ILO's establishment see, inter alia, Rodgers, Lee, Swepston and van Daele, *The ILO and the Quest for Social Justice*, 1919–2009, ILO 2009. Other aspects of the ILO history can be found on the ILO web site http://www.ilo.org, under the Century Project.

Institutionally, it was part of the League of Nations, though it had a separate existence and the two organizations gradually grew apart.

At its first Conference in 1919, the ILO began the task of adopting international labor legislation in the form of Conventions and Recommendations on various questions. Among the instruments adopted in this first period of the ILO were conventions on child labor, protection of women in the work place and forced labor, all of which will be dealt with below. With the outbreak of World War II, the League of Nations met its end but the ILO survived. It was reanimated with the adoption of the Declaration of Philadelphia in 1944, restating and modernising its aims, which was incorporated into the ILO Constitution in 1946. The Declaration expanded the field of action of the ILO, based on the relationship between labor and economic, social and financial questions. Its renewed mandate was stated in the Declaration in terms of human values and aspirations, prefiguring the human rights language the nascent United Nations was soon to adopt: "all human beings, irrespective of race, creed or sex, have the right to pursue both their material well-being and their spiritual development in conditions of freedom and dignity, of economic security and equal opportunity".[5] The ILO became the first specialized agency of the United Nations system in 1945.

2 *Structure of the ILO*

There are two main characteristics that distinguish the ILO from other intergovernmental organizations—its tripartite structure and its standards. The ILO has a unique structure among international organizations. It is an intergovernmental organization, but its decision-making bodies are tripartite. This means that all ILO bodies—with a few exceptions—are composed of representatives of workers and employers as well as governments. As the Constitution states, the annual conference 'shall be composed of four representatives of each of the Members, of whom two shall be Government delegates and the two others shall be delegates representing respectively the employers and the workpeople of each of the Members.'[6] Thus, in the plenary of the annual International Labor Conference, as well as in the Governing Body of the International Labor Office, governments have 50% of the vote, and employers and workers 25% each. At the committee level of the Conference, the power is even more divided, with each group having one-third of the total voting power.[7] This pattern has profound implications for the ILO's decision-making

5 ILO Constitution, Declaration of Philadelphia, Part II(a).

6 Article 3(1), ILO Constitution.

7 Article 65 of the General Standing Orders of the International Labor Conference.

structures. It makes the ILO the only inter-governmental body in which governments do not have all the votes, and in which non-governmental organizations are given a formal role in deciding on the organization's policies.

3 *International Labor Standards and Human Rights*

The ILO was created to adopt international standards to improve the situation of working people. It adopts Conventions—binding on countries which ratify them—and Recommendations, a form of instrument unique to the ILO, which have the force of declarations and are indications of best practice. Since the ILO's establishment in 1919 it has adopted 189 Conventions (as of 2013) which have garnered over 7,800 ratifications by member States. Accompanying them are 202 Recommendations, and there are protocols for five Conventions. (These figures change almost every year, as standard setting is a recurrent item on the ILO agenda.)

As will be seen in the chapter on the Right to Work, the League of Nations and the ILO had moved together in 1926 and 1930 respectively to create international standards on slavery and on forced labor, but the human rights aspects of labor law were otherwise almost unexplored until the 1940s. At the end of World War II, as the United Nations was being created, the ILO moved in anticipation of the founding of the United Nations to update its role in the world by the adoption of the Declaration of Philadelphia in 1944, which was incorporated into its Constitution in 1946. The original Constitution of 1919 had taken the position that "lasting universal peace can only be established if it is based upon social justice", and that it was for this reason that working conditions had to be improved. In the Declaration of Philadelphia the ILO moved into human rights territory by stating its aims in terms of human values and aspirations: "all human beings, irrespective of race, creed or sex, have the right to pursue their material well-being and their spiritual development in conditions of freedom and dignity, of economic security and equal opportunity." This launched a period of 12 years of intense human rights standard-setting by the ILO, culminating in 1958, fuelled both by its own imperatives and by UN requests to the ILO. This period saw the adoption by the ILO of its foundation Conventions on freedom of association and collective bargaining, discrimination and indigenous tribal peoples, and of the second instrument on forced labor. ILO standards were, in turn, the basis for the labor-related provisions in the two human rights Covenants adopted by the United Nations in 1966 to translate the Universal Declaration into more binding form. And the instruments the ILO had already adopted also had a profound influence on the Universal Declaration itself.

Since then, the ILO and the United Nations have worked in parallel, and often closely together, to develop international standards of human rights conduct. The relationship is often apparent only to those within the two organizations, with the UN adopting standards of general application, and broad statements of international law, while the ILO develops in much more detail the aspects of those rights which fall within its own mandate.

In addition, the ILO cooperates with the UN's supervisory bodies to promote the implementation of the standards both adopt. It participates regularly in the work of the Human Rights Council, as it once participated in the Commission on Human Rights and its subsidiary bodies, and cooperates very closely with the "treaty bodies" of the United Nations supervising the implementation of the two human rights Covenants and other instruments including those on racial discrimination, women, migrant workers and the rights of the child.

4 *The Supervision of ILO Standards*

The ILO has a uniquely thorough and influential supervisory system,[8] though it has weaknesses as well. When a Convention has been ratified, a government is required to send periodic reports[9] to the International Labor Office. At the same time, each government is required by article 23 of the ILO Constitution to send copies of these reports to the most representative organizations of employers and of workers in the country (often governments send reports to a number of organizations) which in turn have the right to make their own comments upon these reports. Present reporting volume is about 2,000 government reports received a year (from just under 3,000 requested), and over 300 supplementary comments by employers' and workers' organizations.

---

8 Detailed descriptions of the ILO's supervisory machinery can be found in ILO, *Handbook of procedures relating to international labor Conventions and Recommendations* (Rev. 2012), and ILO, *Rules of the Game: a brief introduction to International Labor Standards* (Revised edition 2009), both available on the ILO web site (http://www.ilo.org). See also, e.g., Swepston, *The International Labor Organization and Human Rights*, in *International Protection of Human Rights: A Textbook*, Inst. Hum. Rights (Krause & Scheinen ed., Abo Akademi 2009 (rev. ed. 2012)).

9 The Constitution (article 22) provides that reports be annual. In practice, in order to accommodate the growing number of ratifications, reporting frequency has been modified several times, and reports are now due at intervals of between one and five years. The annual requirement is met by the filing of reports indicating that nothing major has changed pending the next regularly-scheduled detailed report, or out-of-cycle detailed report requested by ILO supervisory bodies.

Governments' reports and the supplementary information available are examined by the *Committee of Experts on the Application of Conventions and Recommendations*, a body of 20 independent experts drawn from the major economic and social systems. They issue an annual report, containing a general report and a large number of *observations*, or published comments. These are supplemented by a much larger number of *direct requests*, which are not published in paper form but are sent directly to governments.[10] These comments by the Committee of Experts contain questions, requests for amendment of national law and practice to come into greater conformity with ratified Conventions, and a great deal of information on the situation in each country. The Committee of Experts also publishes an annual General Survey, which is an examination or one or more Conventions and/or Recommendations on a subject selected by the Governing Body; these are detailed and informative, and examine the state of application of the selected instruments in both ratifying and non-ratifying countries.

The Committee of Experts' report is submitted to the International Labor Conference,[11] where it is discussed by a tripartite Conference Committee on the Application of Standards. This Committee selects from among the observations to invite about 25 governments each year to appear before it to discuss publicly the observations made by the Committee of Experts. Like other ILO supervisory materials, the discussions in the Conference Committee are available in the report of each Conference session on the ILO web site.[12]

The ILO Constitution also allows for two kinds of complaints procedures. Under article 24 of the Constitution, organizations of employers and of workers may make *representations* that a government has not taken measures to ensure the satisfactory observance within its jurisdiction of a Convention it has ratified. This leads to an examination by a tripartite committee of the Governing Body, and the issuance of a report detailing any problems in observance and recommendations for improvement. Article 26 of the Constitution

---

10 A formalistic distinction is maintained by the ILO between publication in the form of a volume—i.e., observations—and making direct requests available on the NORMLEX data base after communicating them directly to the governments concerned. NORMLEX also contains observations, the texts of Conventions and Recommendations and of the Constitution, reports of the Committee on Freedom of Association (see below), reports of the Conference Committee on the Application of Standards, and other supervisory materials. NORMLEX is available on the ILO web site.

11 Report III, Part 1A to each session of the Conference. Published annually by the ILO, and available in electronic form as of about February each year on the ILO web site and search under NORMLEX.

12 To examine these discussions, go to the ILO web site under Labor Standards.

allows for *complaints* to be filed by governments of other countries that have ratified the same Convention, delegates to the International Labor Conference, and the Governing Body itself. A complaint is examined by a special Commission of Inquiry, the ILO's highest investigative body, composed of independent personalities appointed by the Director-General.[13]

Finally, special procedures have been established for freedom of association. By agreement with the United Nations Economic and Social Council in 1950, the tripartite Governing Body *Committee on Freedom of Association* examines complaints of violations of constitutional principles of freedom of association and the right to collective bargaining from workers' and employers' organizations and—theoretically, at least—from governments. This does not depend on the ratification of the related ILO Conventions, but operates on the basis of obligations concerning freedom of association directly under the ILO Constitution—in effect, treating the Constitution as a human rights treaty. The *Fact-Finding and Conciliation Commission on Freedom of Association* is a more formal procedure for examining the same category of complaints, and depends on the consent of the government concerned to proceed. The findings of the Committee on Freedom of Association are summarized in the *Digest of Decisions*,[14] published and periodically updated on the ILO web site. (This is examined in more detail in the chapter on freedom of association.)

This panoply of supervisory procedures has been highly effective, especially compared to other supervisory bodies in the international system. A high rate of reporting, acceptance by almost all States invited to appear before the Conference Committee, and a large number of complaints examined by the Governing Body and the Committee on Freedom of Association attest to a general respect for the procedures. It is also effective in securing modifications of law and practice in member States in a high number of countries, and is generally well respected. The ILO reinforces its supervisory activity by ensuring that its technical cooperation is closely based on its standards, and that no technical assistance is given which would be contrary to those standards.

The system also suffers weaknesses, and work has been going on in many phases over the years to try to strengthen it. Discussions during the 75th Anniversary of the ILO in 1994 led to the launching of a system of reforms, including a pruning of the large number of active standards by revision, "shelving" of certain older standards, and even procedures for abrogation of outdated

---

13 Reports of all concluded representations and complaints available on NORMLEX, *op cit.*

14 *Digest of decisions and principles of the Freedom of Association Committee of the Governing Body of the ILO.* Fifth (revised) edition, 2006.

Conventions.[15] This kind of review of ILO standards is useful when such a large number have been adopted over the years, and some are either outdated (e.g., standards on conditions of work for trimmers and stokers, who shovelled coal on steam-powered merchant ships), or never received significant numbers of ratifications.

Some critics point to the lack of access by non-governmental organizations to the ILO—other than employers' and workers' organizations—and to the absence of individual complaints procedures; unlike the other points mentioned here, these are not on the ILO's agenda for change.

More important than these structural weaknesses are criticisms that the supervisory bodies of the ILO interpret Conventions beyond their statutory power to do so, that they sometimes impose global solutions that are not provided for in the standards concerned, and that they ignore national characteristics that may mean that standards should be applied differently in different economic and social systems. These criticisms are not without merit in many cases. But they may also conceal a decision by ratifying States to violate international standards they simply do not like—for instance, that would require equal treatment for women and minorities, or allow independent trade unions to function.

B The United Nations

As pointed out in the introduction, there have always been some labor-related aspects of human rights in the UN's work even if the UN has not accorded a major place to these questions in its adoption of standards—obviously, this owes much to the work of the ILO.

Even before the UN's establishment, the League of Nations adopted the Slavery Convention, in 1926, which the United Nations updated with a Protocol in 1953. A Supplementary Convention on the Abolition of Slavery, the Slave Trade, and Institutions and Practices Similar to Slavery was adopted by the United Nations in 1956. (None of these instruments, however, has a treaty body to examine its application by ratifying States.) As noted below, the ILO also has adopted instruments on forced and compulsory labor, which develop these concepts and are now the more important instruments in terms of effect.

The United Nations' basic aims, as laid down in Article 1 of its Charter, include:

---

15 This is in addition to the ILO practice of regular revision of standards, which seems to be process unique to the ILO.

> 3. *To achieve international co-operation in solving international problems of an economic, social, cultural or humanitarian character, and in promoting and encouraging respect for human rights and for fundamental freedoms for all without distinction as to race, sex, language or religion.*

This gives the UN a general responsibility for the human rights aspects of labor law. Any real discussion of labor rights in the United Nations must, of course, begin with the *Universal Declaration of Human Rights* itself. As a global restatement of human rights, it is significant that the Universal Declaration did not omit the labor aspects of the question. Aside from the articles on which the present volume is focussing, there are a number of others which touch on labor rights. General provisions, such as Articles 1, 2 and 7 which speak of equality and non-discrimination, cover labor rights as they do other categories of rights. Article 23 is for all practical purposes a concise restatement of labor rights as human rights, as understood in 1948: the right to work, to free choice of employment, to just and favourable conditions of work and protection against unemployment; the right to "equal pay for equal work",[16] to just and favorable remuneration and the right to join and form trade unions. In addition to these wide-ranging provisions, Article 4 on servitude, slavery and the slave trade is a briefer statement of the themes in the Slavery Convention and the Supplementary Convention, and in ILO Convention No. 29. Article 13 on the right to leave and return to one's own country, has an impact on migrant workers. The protection of the right to freedom of peaceful assembly and association is crucial to the protection of the rights of employers and workers to associate and bargain collectively, and to the provisions of the Covenants on these subjects. The right to social security in Article 22 is closely related to workers' rights. Article 26 protects the right to technical and vocational education as well as general education. This demonstrates that work-related rights are woven intimately into the fabric of human rights by the Universal Declaration, and that it in turn introduces into international human rights law the themes taken up in standards adopted by the ILO both before and after the adoption of the Universal Declaration, by the General Assembly and by others outlined below.

---

16 A more limited statement of this right than in the English version of the ILO Constitution, but not in the French version, and it was shortly to be taken further by the ILO—see below concerning equality.

1 *The Covenants*

The first of the UN's major human rights treaties to be adopted was the International Convention on the Elimination of all forms of Racial Discrimination (CERD), adopted in 1965. This instrument will be considered more in detail below. The most important texts in this field after the Universal Declaration in the United Nations' standard-setting for human rights are the International Covenants on Economic, Social and Cultural Rights, and on Civil and Political Rights, adopted in December 1966, and entering into force 10 years later. Both of them incorporate aspects of labor law into the UN's human rights conventions, in spite of the rather artificial separation of the two instruments into different categories of rights. The intent of the United Nations was to codify into binding law the provisions of the Universal Declaration.

The *International Covenant on Civil and Political Rights* (CPR) includes two principal provisions on labor rights. Article 8 on slavery and forced labor again takes up the theme of the Slavery Convention and the provisions in the Universal Declaration, and closely follows ILO Conventions Nos. 29 of 1930 and 105 of 1957 on the same subject. Article 22 consecrates the right to freedom of association and to join trade unions in the general human rights context of the United Nations. These points will be examined more thoroughly when the related subjects are discussed below.

The *International Covenant on Economic, Social and Cultural Rights* is of course much more relevant to international labor law across more of its provisions. Its Articles 6 to 10 in particular translate into the United Nations human rights sphere the provisions of a number of ILO instruments adopted prior to 1966, while developing a human rights approach to some of them that was different from the ILO's more technical approach at the time.

Article 6 of the ESC Covenant lays down the "right to work", giving a human rights approach missing in the ILO's Employment Policy Convention (No. 122) adopted two years earlier in 1964, which speaks rather of the State's obligation to provide conditions for "full, freely-chosen and productive employment". Article 6 goes on to provide for the conditions under which the right to work can be exercised.

Article 7 is a wide-ranging provision touching on working conditions in a number of respects under the general heading of "just and favorable conditions of work". It provides for adequate levels of remuneration, equality for women, safe and healthy working conditions,[17] equal opportunity, and rest, leisure and working hours. A large number of ILO Conventions adopted both

---

17 Article 12(2)(b) of this Covenant refers to "industrial hygiene", which is also an aspect of safe and healthy working conditions.

before and after the Covenant, provide more detailed regulation in international law of the subjects covered in this article, but their inclusion here lends a human rights aspect to these rights.

Article 8 is a more detailed equivalent of Article 22 of the Civil and Political Rights Covenant. It covers freedom of association and trade union rights for workers (but not for employers as do the ILO instruments).

Article 9 provides for the right to social security, which is partly a labor-related right.

Several other articles relate to aspects of labor rights, but are not primarily focussed on this subject. For example, *Article 10* is concerned with family life, protection of maternity and child labor, all of which are relevant to international labor law. *Article 11* recognizes the right to an adequate standard of living. *Article 13* is primarily concerned with education, but refers in para. 2(b) to "technical and vocational secondary education".

The Committee on Economic, Social and Cultural Rights has in recent years shown a marked interest in the labor rights aspects of its provisions, as will be developed in the more detailed discussions below. Its General Comment No. 18 on Article 6 is particularly relevant; and at this writing (early 2013) a General Comment on Article 7 is under consideration.

The Covenants are supervised by the Human Rights Committee (for the CPR Covenant) and the Committee on Economic, Social and Cultural Rights (for the Covenant of the same name). The former was established in the CPR (Article 28), and came into existence with the coming into force of the Covenant in 1976. The Covenant on Economic, Social and Cultural Rights was originally considered less important, however, and under its Article 19 it was originally to be supervised by the Economic and Social Council and the Commission on Human Rights. This provision was never used, however, as a special Committee was created for its supervision by ECOSOC Resolution 1985/17 of 28 May 1985 to carry out the monitoring functions.

2 *Other Basic Human Rights Treaties of the United Nations*

The United Nations has of course adopted many instruments relevant to human rights, but in addition to the two Covenants, a privileged place is given to the conventions that have given rise to "treaty bodies". These instruments are known collectively as the International Bill of Human Rights. Almost all of them have at least some relevance to the labor rights in articles 23 and 24 of the UDHR.

The other UN treaties that are supervised by "treaty bodies" are the 1965 *International Convention on the Elimination of All Forms of Racial Discrimination*, supervised by the Committee on the Elimination of Racial Discrimination

(CERD) created by Article 8 of the Convention; the 1979 *Convention on the Elimination of All Forms of Discrimination against Women*, supervised by the Committee on the Elimination of Discrimination against Women (CEDAW), created in Article 17 of the Convention; the 1984 *Convention against Torture and Other Cruel, Inhuman or Degrading Treatment or Punishment*, supervised by the Committee against Torture (CAT), created in Article 17 of the Convention; the 1989 *Convention on the Rights of the Child*, supervised by the Committee on the Rights of the Child (CRC), created in Article 43 of the Convention); the *International Convention on the Protection of the Rights of All Migrant Workers and Members of their Families*, adopted in 1990, which is supervised by the Committee on the Protection of the Rights of All Migrant Workers and Members of Their Families (CMW), created by Article 72 of the Convention; and the *Convention on the Rights of Persons with Disabilities*, supervised by the Committee on the Rights of Persons with Disabilities (CRPD), created by Article 34 of the Convention.

None of the other United Nations Conventions on human rights have specific supervisory mechanisms, and their implementation is examined—in general terms—by the Human Rights Council, under the Universal Periodic Review mechanism.

Some of these core instruments are specifically on labor-related issues, such as the International Convention on the Protection of the Rights of All Migrant Workers and Members of their Families, but all affect labor rights more or less directly. In some of them—for instance the CRC—labor rights are written into the Conventions specifically, while in others the effects on labor of the Conventions have been developed through supervision. These aspects will be examined below.

C International Financial Institutions

1 *Global IFIs*

It was not originally contemplated that organizations such as the World Bank, the regional development banks and the International Monetary Fund should play a role in international labor law, but their operations have led them more and more into the field.

The international financial institutions—the World Bank Group and the regional development banks in particular—have an often unremarked influence on international human rights law, including international labor law such as that outlined in articles 23 and 24 of the Universal Declaration. These organizations are governed by their own articles of agreement and in many cases have only gradually begun to commit to the social development goals of the rest of the international system. In particular, as concerns labor questions, these institutions have historically been reluctant to promote international labor standards in their work, and in some cases have been unwilling to accept that these agreed international standards should have any influence on their own missions. They nevertheless impose policies on recipient countries that affect such questions as child labor, social security and other workplace policies that ignore the obligations binding on these countries under ratified international standards.

Over the last decade, however, there have been developments at the levels of both policy and implementation in most of them. While these developments have been uneven, and in some cases policies have been adopted without being followed by measures to implement them, there has been a trend toward policy coherence in favor of the basic principles of the ILO.

Among the improvements, in 2010 the International Finance Corporation (IFC)—the private finance arm of the World Bank group—abandoned a ranking system in its *Doing Business* report that scored countries that had the fewest protections for workers as most business friendly.

The most striking positive development in recent years in the relation between international financial institutions and human rights is the adoption by the IFC of *Performance Standards on Environmental and Social Sustainability*.[18] These Performance Standards were adopted in 2006 and a revised version came into force at the beginning of 2012. They set conditionalities for development loans to private enterprise in developing countries that include in Performance Standard 2 a comprehensive statement of labor standards conditions, conforming closely to the fundamental rights espoused by the ILO.

In another positive development, though with limited impact, there is now an agreed text including labor clauses in contracts of over $10 million for procurement of works—i.e., construction—by development banks. While this is a major advance, no such conditions apply to contracts for other purposes or for amounts smaller than $10 million.[19]

18 http://www1.ifc.org/wps/wcm/connect/topics_ext_content/ifc_external_corporate_site/ifc+sustainability/publications/publications_handbook_pps consulted in April 2013.

19 International Federation of Consulting Engineers (FIDIC), Conditions of Contract for Construction: MDB Harmonised Edition, Geneva, 2010. The articles corresponding to CLS requirements are Section VII, articles 6.20, 6.21, 6.23 and 6.24 (pp. 27–28), with other articles relating to more general conditions of work. The participating banks for the MDB Harmonized Major Works Contract are: African Development Bank, Asian Development

The need to ensure that the international institutions working for economic and social development are pursuing common goals has been intensified in the global financial crisis. The ILO has responded in particular by the adoption of the Global Jobs Pact in 2009, and there has been growing agreement on the need for this Pact to be part of the work of all the relevant institutions throughout the United Nations system. In particular, a resolution adopted by the Economic and Social Council in July 2011[20] included the following paragraphs:

> 4. *Recognises* the need to universally respect, promote and realise fundamental principles and rights at work, in accordance with The International Labor Organisation Declaration on Fundamental Principles and Rights at Work;
> 5. *Also recognises* the need to promote and realise at least basic social protection in order to achieve decent work, and a nationally design social protection floors, in all countries, in line with national priorities and circumstances;
> 6. *Welcomes* the efforts by the international financial institutions and other relevant organisations, as well as by the United Nations development system, to integrate into their activities policy measures mentioned in the global jobs pact;

2 *Regional IFIs*

The regional development banks have incorporated labor standards into their operations in widely differing ways.

a EBRD

In May 2008 the European Bank for Reconstruction and Development (EBRD) adopted a revised Environmental and Social Policy,[21] inspired by the IFC, after detailed consultations with the ILO, the IFC and trade unions, among others. This includes a detailed Performance Standard 2 on Labor and Working

---

Bank, Black Sea Trade and Development Bank, Caribbean Development Bank, Council of Europe Development Bank, European Bank for Reconstruction and Development, Inter-American Development Bank and World Bank. See also International Trade Union Confederation (ITUC), *Labor Standards in World Bank Group Lending: Lessons Learned and Next Steps*, 2011.

20 ECOSOC resolution E/2011/L21/Rev1.

21 See http://www.ebrd.com/pages/research/publications/policies/environmental.shtml. Consulted 26 May 2013.

Conditions. This is now the most advanced of the IFIs' social policies. PS2 includes the following:

> 1. *EBRD believes that for any business, the workforce is a valuable asset, and that good human resources management and a sound worker-management relationship based on respect for workers' rights, including freedom of association and right to collective bargaining, are key ingredients to the sustainability of the enterprise. By treating workers fairly and providing them with safe and healthy working conditions, clients may create tangible benefits, such as enhancement of the efficiency and productivity of their operations. Conversely, failure to establish and foster a sound worker/management relationship can undermine worker commitment and retention, jeopardise a project and damage the client's reputation.*
>
> ....
>
> 7. *Projects are required to comply, at a minimum, with:*
>   - *national labor, social security and occupational health and safety laws, and*
>   - *ILO conventions related to:*
>   *a) the abolition of child labor*
>   *b) the elimination of forced labor*
>   *c) the elimination of discrimination related to employment*
>   *d) the freedom of association and collective bargaining.*

The Performance Standard goes on to list requirements for wages, benefits and conditions of work, occupational safety and health, retrenchment, grievance mechanisms and supply chains.

b Inter-American Development Bank

There is no broad, programmatic commitment to labor standards in the IADB. In February 2006 the IADB adopted guidelines on "Managing Labor Issues In Infrastructure Projects",[22] applicable to the private sector, that include extensive references to ILO standards. It goes well beyond the core standards, and deals also with other aspects of conditions of work, but little is known about its application in practice. In fact, it closely resembles, and appears to have been overtaken by, the agreement on standardized bidding clauses adopted in 2010 by all the major IFIs—see above.

---

22 See http://www.iadb.org/en/publications/publication-detail,7101.html?id=42286. Consulted 26 May 2013.

The Inter-American Investment Corporation, the private sector lending facility (which is analogous to the World Bank's IFC) does have a policy that refers to labor standards, the Procedure for Environmental and Labor Review of IIC Projects, dated 1999. This policy appears, however, to be largely in abeyance.

c Asian Development Bank

The ADB adopted a commitment to core labor standards as part of its Social Protection Strategy in 2001; and in 2006 the ADB published a **Core Labor Standards Handbook**[23] that was co-authored by the ILO. It appears, however, that the commitment to labor standards in ADB operations was never implemented. The ILO and the ADB do continue to affirm that core labor standards should be promoted, but as of this writing (2013) there is no identifiable operational policy on this subject.[24]

d African Development Bank

There is no evidence that the AfDB has considered formally the issue of incorporating labor standards into its planning and operations. The African Development Bank is covered by the standard bidding forms for large-scaled infrastructure projects.

D Regional Organizations

1 *Europe*

The most highly developed regional system that makes labor standards applicable to member countries, is that of Europe. It differs significantly from the universal systems in that the international conventions adopted on the regional level actually become binding in the internal law of Member States, and enforceable under many circumstances. It is in this respect not strictly comparable to other international regimes, and has in many respects created a regional legislature rather than a treaty system. This makes it, of course, all the more effective in giving substance to the Universal Declaration, when working in the field of human rights.

The ***European Convention for the Protection of Human Rights and Fundamental Freedoms*** (*also known as the European Convention on Human*

---

23 See http://www.adb.org/documents/core-labor-standards-handbook. Consulted 26 May 2013.

24 See http://www.adb.org/news/adb-ilo-reaffirm-support-core-labor-standards. Consulted 26 May 2013.

Rights) was adopted in 1950, just two years after the Universal Declaration, and entered into force in 1953. It covers many of the same rights as the Universal Declaration and the UN and ILO Conventions mentioned above. A number of protocols have been adopted to supplement its original provisions, most notably for the purposes of the present volume in 1998. The Convention created the *European Court of Human Rights*, which hears complaints from a number of sources.[25]

The ***European Social Charter*** was adopted in 1961 and revised in 1996. It goes into greater detail than the European Convention in the social field covered by the present volume. Its implementation is supervised by the European Committee of Social Rights.

2 *The Americas*

On 2 May 1948—five months before the adoption of the Universal Declaration of Human Rights—the Ninth International Conference of American States adopted the *American Declaration of the Rights and Duties of Man*. The American Declaration prefigures much of the language and concepts that were shortly afterwards to be adopted in the Universal Declaration.

The ***American Convention on Human Rights***, known also as the "Pact of San José", was adopted on 22 November 1969, and entered into force in 1978.

The American Convention contains many of the rights enshrined in the articles of the Universal Declaration which are being examined here, as will be seen below. It adopts the unusual approach of distinguishing within the text between civil and political rights (Chapter II, articles 3 to 25) and economic, social and cultural rights (Chapter III, article 26). The Convention was adopted three years after the two International Covenants on Human Rights adopted by the United Nations, but it is evident from the actual contents of the American Convention that the distinction drawn between these two "kinds" of rights had already eroded considerably: the single article on economic, social and cultural rights merely commits signatories to implementing those rights contained in the OAS Charter. This was, however, recognized as inadequate, and the Additional Protocol in the area of Economic, Social and Cultural Rights was adopted in 1988, and entered into force in 1999.

The Convention vests supervisory powers in the Inter-American Commission on Human Rights[26] (which was established in 1960) and in the Inter-American Court of Human Rights.[27]

---

25 Articles 19 to 51.

26 Chapter VII, Articles 34 to 51.

27 Chapter VIII, Articles 52 *et seq.*

The *Inter-American Commission on Human Rights* has the power to receive complaints from individuals and NGOs about violations of the Convention, to make recommendations to member States and to report to the OAS Conference or the Meeting of Consultation on the situation in particular countries. It has seven members, elected in a purely personal capacity. Under the Convention, cases can be referred to the Court by either the Inter-American Commission on Human Rights or a state party. States must have accepted the jurisdiction of the Court for it to be able to examine cases. In contrast to the European human rights system, individual citizens of the OAS member states are not allowed to take cases directly to the Court.

3 *Africa*

The *African Charter on Human and Peoples' Rights* was adopted by the Organization of African Unity in 1981, and came into force in 1986. It follows the general lines laid down in other conventions in regard to the rights proclaimed in the Universal Declaration but—as will be seen below in examining the different standards in detail—with a different approach in many ways.

The Charter creates[28] the *African Commission on Human and Peoples' Rights*, "within the Organization of African Unity to promote human and peoples' rights and ensure their protection in Africa." (article 30). The Commission consists of eleven independent persons, which is to have a promotional role as well as being empowered to receive communications. Unfortunately, the Commission has never really begun functioning as designed, in spite of real efforts by its officials, because of lack of financial and other support by the member States.

4 *Arab countries*

The Arab Labor Organization was established by the League of Arab States in 1965. Its Headquarters is in Cairo, after having departed from that country following the Camp David Peace Agreements, and then returned. Its structure and aims are similar to those of the ILO, and it also has adopted labor Conventions (which have somewhat lower standards than the comparable ILO instruments).

The League of Arab States drew up an Arab Convention on Labor Standards in 1967.[29] This Convention is based closely on ILO Conventions adopted by that time, and it provides that it shall not affect any Conventions or international treaties that are more favourable to the beneficiaries. The convention

---

28 Part II, articles 30 to 59.

29 See ILO *Legislative Series*, 1967–Int. 1.

covers the following subjects: vocational training, employment and mobility of workers, individual contracts of employment, wages, hours of work, health protection and the prevention of employment accidents, protection of young persons, protection of women workers, social protection, labor-management co-operation, workers' unions and employers' organizations, settlement of labor disputes, labor administration, labor inspection, labor courts and social insurance.

The convention also provides, in Part III, for the Application of the Convention. Ratifying states are required to accept at least 51 of the 99 substantive articles of the Convention, and may increase this number over time.[30] Annual reports are to be supplied to the Secretary-General of the Arab League on the application of the Articles by which the country is bound (Article 111), copies of which are to be sent to employers' and workers' organizations (Article 113). The reports are to be examined by a committee of experts (Article 114), appointed by the Ministers of Labor "from among candidates nominated by the Contracting Parties" (Art. 115). The committee of experts submits its report to an annual meeting of the Arab Ministers of Labor; and the Ministers "shall draw up a report containing their recommendations, which shall be submitted to the Council of the Arab League for action" (Article 117). It does not appear that this supervisory system actually functions.

5 *Asia*

There is no regional system in Asia to deal with human rights issues. In 2012 the Association of South East Asia States (ASEAN) adopted the first regional commitment to human rights, the ASEAN Human Rights Declaration. It is nearly free of any commitments on human rights in the workplace, apart from the following general statements in Art. 27:

> 27. (1) Every person has the right to work, to the free choice of employment, to enjoy just, decent and favourable conditions of work and to have access to assistance schemes for the unemployed.
>
> (2) Every person has the right to form trade unions and join the trade union of his or her choice for the protection of his or her interests, in accordance with national laws and regulations.
>
> (3) No child or any young person shall be subjected to economic and social exploitation. Those who employ children and young people in work harmful to their morals or health, dangerous to life, or likely to hamper their normal development, including their education should be

30 Arab Labor Convention, Art. 110.

> punished by law. ASEAN Member States should also set age limits below which the paid employment of child labor should be prohibited and punished by law.

E Trade Agreements and Labor Standards[31]

There was a long push by some of the developed countries, particularly the United States, the United Kingdom and Canada, to install a so-called 'social clause' into the machinery of international trade regulation. This attempt, warmly supported by the international trade union movement, was intended to make trade privileges, in particular reduced import tariffs, dependent on respect for basic labor standards. Such a clause was included in the founding documents of the International Trade Organization that was to be established in the 1950s by the Havana Charter, but that Organization never came into existence.[32] Discussions of a possible social clause were raised also under the General Agreement on Trade and Tariffs (GATT). Exporting countries, however, systematically rejected these moves, which they said were purely protectionist in intent and would take away their competitive advantage based in lower labor costs.

With the establishment of the World Trade Organization under discussion, a certain number of countries attempted to insert a requirement for respect of labor rights into the new Organization, but this attempt was firmly rejected by the majority in the Singapore Declaration of Ministers in 1996. As concerns Core Labor Standards, that Declaration stated in paragraph 4:[33]

> We renew our commitment to the observance of internationally recognized core labor standards. The International Labor Organization (ILO) is the competent body to set and deal with these standards, and we affirm our support for its work in promoting them. We believe that economic growth and development fostered by increased trade and further trade

---

31 See Doumbia-Henry and Gravel, *Free trade agreements and labor rights: Recent developments*, International Labor Review, Vol. 145 (2006), No. 3; and ILO, *Social Dimensions of Free Trade Agreements*, 2013 (available on the ILO web site).

32 See the description of the history of the World Trade Organization, including the abortive attempt to establish the International Trade Organization, at http://www.wto.org/english/thewto_e/whatis_e/tif_e/fact4_e.htm.

33 Singapore WTO Ministerial 1996: MINISTERIAL DECLARATION WT/MIN(96)/DEC, 18 December 1996 (see the web site of the World Trade Organization, at http://www.wto.org/english/thewto_e/minist_e/min96_e/wtodec_e.htm, consulted 22 April 2013.)

> liberalization contribute to the promotion of these standards. We reject the use of labor standards for protectionist purposes, and agree that the comparative advantage of countries, particularly low-wage developing countries, must in no way be put into question. In this regard, we note that the WTO and ILO Secretariats will continue their existing collaboration.

This was understood by all concerned to remove consideration of labor standards from the future work of the WTO and refer it to the ILO, and this has continued to be the case. It helped pave the way for the adoption by the ILO of the Declaration of Fundamental Principles and Rights at Work in 1998. Article 5 of that Declaration reflected the continuing concerns by a number of developing exporting countries with the following language:

> Stresses that labor standards should not be used for protectionist trade purposes, and that nothing in this Declaration and its follow-up shall be invoked or otherwise used for such purposes; in addition, the comparative advantage of any country should in no way be called into question by this Declaration and its follow-up.

This in turn was balanced 10 years later with the following provision of the Social Justice Declaration by the ILO:[34]

> ... that the violation of fundamental principles and rights at work cannot be invoked or otherwise used as a legitimate comparative advantage and that labor standards should not be used for protectionist trade purposes.

Thwarted in attempts to insert respect for labor standards into multilateral agreements, the United States, the European Union and Canada began promoting trade agreements with developing countries promising them access to the markets of developing countries under favorable conditions, while imposing conditionalities of respect for labor standards in their bilateral trade agreements—and in some cases multilateral agreements with defined commercial blocks. These typically lay down standards or principles to be respected in a 'Generalized system of preferences', and balance this requirement with guarantees to help improve labor standards in developing countries.[35]

---

34 ILO Declaration on Social Justice for a Fair Globalization, 2008, section I(A)(iv).

35 For the United States, see the web site of the US Trade Representative, at http://www.ustr.gov/trade-agreements (consulted April 2013).

The restricted multilateral trade agreements to which reference is made above include the North American Free Trade Agreement (NAFTA), concluded in 1993 among Canada, Mexico and the United States. It includes a North American Agreement on Labor Co-operation, with a special procedure for monitoring national labor standards, under which all the countries concerned agree to work to implement fully their own labor legislation. The 2004 *Dominican Republic-Central America-United States Free Trade Agreement* (*CAFTA-DR*) includes a commitment by which:

> 1. The Parties reaffirm their obligations as members of the International Labor Organization (ILO) and their commitments under the *ILO Declaration on Fundamental Principles and Rights at Work and its Follow-Up (1998)* (ILO Declaration). Each Party shall strive to ensure that such labor principles and the internationally recognized labor rights set forth in Article 16.8 are recognized and protected by its law.

Other such regional agreements may follow, and they are likely to include language similar to that quoted here, committing the parties to observe core ILO standards—which for the purposes of this volume constitutes also a commitment to observe parts of the Universal Declaration of Human Rights.

Bilateral trade agreements have also been concluded between the United States and a number of other nations, and they promote the observance of labor standards as a precondition to favorable trade relations.[36]

The Generalised System of Preference in force in the European Union includes what is referred to as 'GSP+'. The "GSP+" enhanced preferences means full removal of tariffs on a range of product categories, granted to countries which ratify and implement international conventions relating to human and labor rights, environment and good governance.[37]

---

36 Ibid.

37 The EU adopted a reformed GSP law on 31 October 2012 (Regulation No 978/2012). See the European Commission web page on Trade, at http://ec.europa.eu/trade/policy/countries-and-regions/development/generalised-scheme-of-preferences/index_en.htm. (Consulted 27 May 2013.)

CHAPTER 2

Implementation of the Provisions of the Universal Declaration

In what follows, the implementation through international law of Articles 23 and 24 of the Universal Declaration will be examined. This will include ILO standards and supervision, UN Conventions and action by their respective treaty bodies, and action by other bodies at the universal and regional levels.

In so far as comments of supervisory bodies goes, it must be taken into account that the material here is valid up to November 2013, when the present volume was submitted for publication. Naturally, these bodies continue to work, and may supplement or amend their positions from time to time.

Article 23

This examination of the implementation of the Universal Declaration will take Articles 23 and 24 phrase by phrase, and examine how each of the rights provided for is implemented in law and in practice.

Article 23 (1) provides:

> *Everyone has the right to work, to free choice of employment, to just and favourable conditions of work and protection against unemployment.*

 | DOI 10.1163/9789004244559_005

A Everyone has the Right to Work …

The first thing to make clear is that the *right to work* is not understood as a right to a job, but rather as the right to have the conditions created under which it is possible to find work—this is elaborated below.

The right to work is for some, the "right" that makes it difficult to take human rights seriously as a concept, since it assigns the status of a "right" to something that cannot effectively be guaranteed by States in all conditions. Others have considered this to be the pre-eminent right in the economic field, for how can the others be enjoyed if this one is not assured? The *Encyclopaedia universalis* states that the phrase "the right to work" originated with Charles Fourier (1772–1837) who declared that "politics extol the rights of man and do not guarantee the prime and only useful right, the right to work."[38] At about the same time, a diametrically opposed argument was being made by de Tocqueville during the debates on the right to work in the French Constituent Assembly of 1848:

> To grant to every man … (the) right to work necessarily leads to one of the following consequences: either the State will undertake to give to all workers applying to it the employment they lack and will then be gradually drawn into industry … Now that is communism. If, on the contrary, the State wishes … to provide employment to all the workers who seek it … to see that they will always find work with private employers, it will inevitably be lead to try to regulate industry … in a word, … it will have to become the great and only organizer of labor … What do we see? Socialism.[39]

These two visions from some of the earliest modern debates on human rights indicate the central place of this concept in human rights, and the confusion and uncertainty it has always aroused.

From the point of view of protection of rights, this treatment of the right to work leaves one feeling somewhat unsatisfied. This is a general problem with this kind of treatment in international law, which can evaluate process and outcomes on a general level, but cannot focus on individual claims to the protection of a right to work.

---

38 Encyclopaedia universalis (Paris, 1968–75) vol. 16, article "Travail", p. 276.

39 Ibid., vol. 5, article "Droits de l'homme", p. 819. Both quotes, and much of the rest of the material in this section, is drawn from Mayer, Jean, "The concept of the right to work in international standards and the legislation of ILO member States", *International Labor Review*, Vol. 124, No. 2, March–April 1985.

It will be seen from what follows that this is a subject in which the impact of rights instruments leaves rights advocates dissatisfied. Unlike the content and supervision of international organizations concerning individual rights for which remedies are available, the best that can be hoped for in this field is that governments feel that attention continues to be focussed on the impact on their own populations of their economic policies—an awareness that there are rights implications of economic decisions even if this is not ultimately what moves these decisions. Elsewhere in this volume it can be seen that focus on human rights has had an impact on the behavior of States; in respect of the right to work, it is certainly economic efficiency that comes before thoughts of rights when employment policy is reviewed.

1 *International Instruments*

a The United Nations

The International Covenant on Economic, Social and Cultural Rights incorporated the expression of the right to work in Article 6, providing considerable content to the bare statement contained in the Universal Declaration:

> 1. *The States Parties to the present Covenant recognize the right to work, which includes the right of everyone to the opportunity to gain his living by work which he freely chooses or accepts, and will take the appropriate steps to safeguard this right.*
> 2. *The steps to be taken by a State Party to the present Covenant to achieve the full realization of this right shall include technical and vocational guidance and training programmes, policies and techniques to achieve steady economic, social and cultural development and full and productive employment under conditions safeguarding fundamental political and economic freedoms to the individual.*

This clearly indicates that the right to work is not a simple guarantee of a job, and that measures will have to be taken at the national level to create a situation in which it can be realized.

ICESCR General Comment on the Right to Work. The Committee on Economic, Social and Cultural Rights adopted General Comment No. 18 on the right to work in 2005, at its 35th Session.[40] As the Committee states:

> 1 ....The right to work is essential for realizing other human rights and forms an inseparable and inherent part of human dignity. Every

40 See UN Doc. HRI/GEN/1/Rev.9 (Vol. I), pp. 139 *et seq*.

individual has the right to be able to work, allowing him/her to live in dignity. The right to work contributes at the same time to the survival of the individual and to that of his/her family, and insofar as work is freely chosen or accepted, to his/her development and recognition within the community.

2. The ICESCR proclaims the right to work in a general sense in its article 6 and explicitly develops the individual dimension of the right to work through the recognition in article 7 of the right of everyone to the enjoyment of just and favourable conditions of work, in particular the right to safe working conditions. The collective dimension of the right to work is addressed in article 8, which enunciates the right of everyone to form trade unions and join the trade union of his/her choice as well as the right of trade unions to function freely. When drafting article 6 of the Covenant, the Commission on Human Rights affirmed the need to recognize the right to work in a broad sense by laying down specific legal obligations rather than a simple philosophical principle.

In paragraph 3, the General Comment describes how the notion of the right to work has figured in other United Nations instruments.

> At the universal level, the right to work is contained in article 8, paragraph 3 (a), of the International Covenant on Civil and Political Civil Rights (ICCPR); in article 5, paragraph (e) (i), of the International Convention on the Elimination of All Forms of Racial Discrimination; in article 11, paragraph 1 (a), of the Convention on the Elimination of All Forms of Discrimination against Women; in article 32 of the Convention on the Rights of the Child;[41] and in articles 11, 25, 26, 40, 52 and 54 of the International Convention on the Protection of the Rights of All Migrant Workers and Members of Their Families. Several regional instruments recognize the right to work in its general dimension, including the European Social Charter of 1961 and the Revised European Social Charter of 1996 (Part II, art. 1), the African Charter on Human and Peoples' Rights (art. 15) and the Additional Protocol to the American Convention on Human Rights in the Area of Economic, Social and Cultural Rights

41 This is a dubious interpretation of the right to be free from economic exploitation. The Convention on the Rights of the Child takes the position in Article 32 that if young people do work it should be in favorable conditions, rather than establishing the morally and legally dangerous position that children have the right to work.

> (art. 6), and affirm the principle that respect for the right to work imposes on States parties an obligation to take measures aimed at the realization of full employment. Similarly, the right to work has been proclaimed by the United Nations General Assembly in the Declaration on Social Progress and Development, in its resolution 2542 (XXIV) of 11 December 1969 (art. 6).

To this list should be added article 27 of the Convention on the Rights of Persons with Disabilities (2006), adopted the year after the General Comment was formulated.

It is important to emphasize that the General Comment makes it clear in its paragraph 6 that:

> The right to work is an individual right that belongs to each person and is at the same time a collective right. It encompasses all forms of work, whether independent work or dependent wage-paid work. *The right to work should not be understood as an absolute and unconditional right to obtain employment.* (emphasis added)

The right to work is therefore a right to demand of the State that it create the conditions under which everyone has access to work, rather than that the State guarantee work to every individual.

b The International Labor Organization

It might be thought that the ILO would be the first to protect the "right to work", but it has not included this phrase in any of its Conventions. However, in line with its normal practice of including in its instruments obligations on governments rather than the rights of those affected, the ILO adopted the *Employment Policy Convention, 1964 (No. 122)*, two years before the Covenants were adopted. Article 1 of this Convention states:

> 1. *With a view to stimulating economic growth and development, raising levels of living, meeting manpower requirements and overcoming unemployment and underemployment, each Member shall declare and pursue, as a major goal, an active policy designed to promote full, productive and freely-chosen employment.*
> 2. *The said policy shall aim at ensuring that—*
>   (*a*) *there is work for all who are available for and seeking work;*
>   (*b*) *such work is as productive as possible;*
>   (*c*) *there is free choice of employment . . .*

It was 20 years after the adoption of Convention No. 122 before the ILO adopted specific language on the right to work, in the Employment Policy (Supplementary Provisions) Recommendation, 1984 (No. 169), which provides in its first two Paragraphs:

> 1. *The promotion of full, productive and freely-chosen employment provided for in the Employment Policy Convention and Recommendation, 1964, should be regarded as the means of achieving in practice the realisation of the right to work.*
> 2. *Full recognition by Members of the right to work should be linked with the implementation of economic and social policies, the purpose of which is the promotion of full, productive and freely-chosen employment.*

This is consistent with the reports the ILO had been submitting to the UN Committee on Economic, Social and Cultural Rights in the on-going collaboration between the two bodies. The ILO had stated that although the Employment Policy Convention did not explicitly mention the right to work, the measures for the realisation of that right provided for in Article 6 (2) of the Covenant were measures of employment policy of the same nature as those called for by the Convention.[42]

2 *Regional Instruments*

a Europe

The *European Convention on Human Rights* contains no provisions on this subject, but the *European Social Charter*, adopted in 1961, contains two provisions. In Part 1, Article 1, the Charter states that: *Everyone shall have opportunity to earn his living in an occupation freely entered upon.* A more substantial provision appears as Article 1 of Part II, in an article entitled "The right to work."

> *With a view to ensuring the effective exercise of the right to work, the Contracting Parties undertake:*
> 1. to accept as one of their primary aims and responsibilities the achievement and maintenance of as high and stable a level of employment as possible, with a view to the attainment of full employment;

42 See, e.g., Report by the Committee of Experts on the Application of Conventions and Recommendations of the International Labor Organisation on progress in achieving observance of the provisions of Articles 6 to 9 of the International Covenant on Economic, Social and Cultural Rights, UN document E/1978/27, para. 18.

2. to protect effectively the right of the worker to earn his living in an occupation freely agreed upon;
3. to establish or maintain free employment services for all workers;
4. to provide or promote appropriate vocational guidance, training and rehabilitation.

b The Americas

The *American Declaration of the Rights and Duties of Man*, adopted some months before the Universal Declaration in 1948, provides as follows in its Article 14:

> *Every person has the right to work, under proper conditions, and to follow his vocation freely, in so far as existing conditions of employment permit.*

This right was not carried over into the 1969 *American Convention on Human Rights*, but when the *Additional Protocol on Economic, Social and Cultural Rights* was adopted in 1988, it included the following at Article 6:

> 1. *Everyone has the right to work, which includes the opportunity to secure the means for living a dignified and decent existence by performing a freely elected or accepted lawful activity.*
> 2. *The States Parties undertake to adopt measures that will make the right to work fully effective, especially with regard to the achievement of full employment, vocational guidance and the development of technical and vocational training projects, in particular those directed to the disabled. The States Parties also undertake to implement and strengthen programs that help to ensure suitable family care, so that women may enjoy a real opportunity to exercise the right to work.*

c Africa

The *African Charter on Human and Peoples' Rights* does not include a direct statement of the right to work, but in Article 15 it does provide for the conditions under which work should be carried out, when it states:

> *Every individual shall have the right to work under equitable and satisfactory conditions, and shall receive equal pay for equal work.*

3 *International Supervision*

The supervisory bodies of both the United Nations and the ILO express concern over the implementation of the right to work, by examining the rates of unemployment and underemployment of the national population and by asking governments to do more to create the conditions under which jobs are created and made available. A second dominant theme is equal opportunity and treatment for all segments of the national population.

a United Nations

The UN Committee on Economic, Social and Cultural Rights frequently examines the employment situation in reporting countries with reference to the right to work, and also tends to concentrate on the situation of excluded minorities who are in a worse employment situation than the rest of the population. The following extract from the concluding observations for one country in 2012 is typical of the kinds of comments made:

> 11. The Committee is concerned, particularly in the context of the economic and financial crisis, about the recent rise in unemployment and long-term unemployment rates, which negatively affect the population of the State party, especially young persons, immigrants, Roma persons and persons with disabilities, and increases their vulnerability in violation of their rights set out in the Covenant (arts. 2, para. 2 and 6).
>
> The Committee recommends that the State party strengthen its programmes and adopt effective strategies to reduce unemployment rates and move progressively towards the full realization of the right to work, avoiding any retrogressive step with regard to the protection of workers' labor rights. The Committee recommends that high-quality vocational training, especially for the long-term unemployed, continue to be prioritized taking into account the needs of disadvantaged and marginalized individuals and groups. The Committee further recommends the adoption of employment strategies and plans of action targeting regions where unemployment is most severe. It also requests the State party, in its next periodic report, to submit tables of annual statistics on the general employment situation, disaggregated by sex, age, nationality, disability, and by urban or rural region. In that regard, the Committee draws the State party's attention to its general comment No. 18 (2005) on the right to work. The Committee also draws the State party's attention to its open letter of 16 May 2012 to States parties on economic, social and cultural rights in the context of the economic and financial crisis.[43]

---

43 Committee on Economic, Social and Cultural Rights, Concluding observations on the combined fourth and fifth reports of Bulgaria, adopted by the Committee at its forty-ninth session (12–30 November 2012), UN doc. E/C.12/BGR/CO/4–5.

The Committee makes similar comments to a large number of countries. The following 2012 comment is a further illustration of the fact that the Committee views the right to work in the context of other rights protected in the Covenant, with particular attention to the right to equal treatment:

> 9. The Committee is concerned that the unemployment rate remains high, despite a decrease in the past decade, and that the informal economy is estimated to represent more than 90 per cent of the overall economy. It is also concerned that the proportion of women among wage earners is low, constituting only about 30 per cent of paid employees (art. 6).
>
> The Committee recommends that the State party increase its efforts to combat unemployment through specifically targeted measures. It recommends that the State party take measures to regularize the situation of informal sector workers by progressively improving their working conditions and including them in social security schemes. The Committee also recommends that the State party take measures to increase the access of women to employment in the formal sector, in particular those living in rural areas.[44]

b International Labor Organization

The ILO's consideration of substantially the same issues is carried out under the Employment Policy Convention, 1964 (No. 122), to which reference is made above. As one of the ILO's priority Conventions, reports are due on it every 3 years from the 108 countries which have ratified the Convention (as of November 2013), and the Committee of Experts makes a number of comments on the Convention's application each year. The Conference Committee on the Application of Standards often discusses one or more of these cases in its annual session. The example below, which concerns Honduras, is from the 2012 report of the Committee of Experts, and the Session of the International Labor Conference that took place later that same year.

The observation concerned, which followed an earlier discussion in the Conference Committee, took note of 'a new and very informative report from the Government received in September 2011, as well as supplementary data provided in November 2011.' The Committee of Experts noted detailed information provided on the Government's employment objectives, and invited it to continue to provide information. It also noted, however, that

44 Concluding observations on the initial to third reports of the United Republic of Tanzania, adopted by the Committee at its forty-ninth session (12–30 November 2012), UN Doc. E/C.12/TZA/CO/1–3.

> In their communication of March 2011 the trade union organizations reported that they were not consulted in November 2010 when the National Congress approved the National Hourly Employment Programme. According to the organizations, the programme proposes to deregulate the labor market, which will deepen precarious employment. The labor market is saturated with temporary and contract workers, and the organizations make the point that abusive employers have no need of a specific programme in order to hire temporary workers. The CUTH indicates that there is no State employment policy for the creation of meaningful and decent jobs.

This observation of the Committee of Experts was followed up by a discussion in the tripartite Conference Committee on the Application of Standards in 2012. After a long exchange all of which is reproduced in detail in the report of the Committee (published in the Proceedings of the Conference), the Conference Committee adopted conclusions that included the following language:

> The Committee noted that the Government reiterated its commitment to the generation of productive employment in the framework of its plans and programmes designed to overcome the difficult situation of underemployment which represents over 40 per cent of the economically active population. The Government also expressed its intention to reform its education and training system to ensure decent job opportunities for young people. It referred to the consultations held with the social partners in the Economic and Social Council and the National Congress to enlist their support with regard to the implementation of the National Solidarity Plan for Anti-crisis Employment.
>
> ...
>
> The Committee invited the Government to report in detail for the next session of the Committee of Experts with an update of the information provided on new measures and their objectives and on the size and distribution of the work-force, as well as specific information on the effectiveness of the measures implemented in reducing underemployment and achieving the objectives of the Convention. The Committee also requested the Government to provide detailed information on how tripartite mechanisms had contributed to the formulation of employment programmes and to the monitoring and implementation of active labor

> market measures in order to overcome the current crisis and to ensure a sustainable recovery.[45]

This one set of comments from the ILO supervisory bodies is fairly typical of the kinds of comments they make on the application of Convention No. 122, and a number more expressing similar concerns are available on the ILO web site. It is worth mentioning that governments that request assistance from the International Labor Office in crafting and implementing their employment promotion strategies usually receive such assistance.

45 Record of Proceedings, International Labor Conference, 101st session, Geneva, June 2012. Provisional Record 18, Part II, p. 94. Available on the ILO web site, http://www.ilo.org.

B Everyone has the Right to . . . Free Choice of Employment

This right has two aspects. The first is the right to be *free from compulsion* concerning work; while this is developed more fully under Article 4 of the Universal Declaration, it needs to be examined here as well as an aspect of workers' rights. The second aspect concerns the right *to have a choice* about the kind of employment each individual must accept, and the corresponding obligation on the State to facilitate that ability to choose.

1 *Freedom from Compulsion—Slavery and Forced Labor*

Slavery and forced and compulsory labor, which are covered more comprehensively under Article 4 of the Declaration,[46] impose violations of human rights on more than the choice of whether or not to undertake work. They also restrict the choice of work one performs. The modern movement in international law for the abolition of slavery and forced labor began with the British Empire's interdiction in 1833 of the slave trade anywhere in the world, and slavery was abolished legally in most countries before the First World War. The year of the 50th anniversary of the Universal Declaration (1998) was also the 150th anniversary of the abolition of slavery in France's colonies. It should not be imagined, however, that this scourge has vanished from the face of the Earth—it still thrives in different forms in many places.

a The League of Nations and the United Nations

i *The Slavery Conventions*

The **Slavery Convention**[47] was adopted in 1926 under the aegis of the League of Nations, and remains in force today. This Convention defines "slavery" as "the status or condition of a person over whom any or all of the powers attaching to the right of ownership are exercised," and goes on to define what it means by the "slave trade."[48] It requires ratifying States to "prevent and suppress the slave trade" and to "bring about, progressively and as soon as possible, the complete abolition of slavery in all its forms."[49]

---

46 Article 4 provides: *No one shall be held in slavery or servitude; slavery and the slave trade shall be prohibited in all their forms.*

47 Signed at Geneva on 25 September 1926. Entry into force: 9 March 1927. The texts of all the United Nations Conventions cited in this work can be consulted on the home page of the Office of the High Commissioner for Human Rights http://www.ohchr.org.

48 Slavery Convention, Article 1.

49 Ibid., Article 2.

Supplementary Convention on the Abolition of Slavery, the Slave Trade, and Institutions and Practices Similar to Slavery.[50] This Convention was adopted in 1956 and entered into force in 1957. It recognized in its preamble that progress had been made since the 1926 Convention, referred to ILO Convention No. 29 (see below), but noted that slavery, the slave trade and institutions similar to slavery "have not yet been eliminated in all parts of the world." This Convention also has no dedicated supervisory mechanism.

The Supplementary Convention required States Parties to "take all practicable and necessary legislative and other measures" to abolish completely four practices:

(a) debt bondage, or "the status or condition arising from a pledge by a debtor of his personal services or those of a person under his control as security for a debt";
(b) serfdom, "the condition or status of a tenant who is by law, custom or agreement bound to live and labor on land belonging to another person and to render some … service";
(c) any institution or practice involving the compulsory marriage of women against payment, the right to transfer a woman to another person, or the possibility that a woman be "inherited by another person" on the death of her husband; and
(d) the transfer of a child under 18 years old to another "with a view to the exploitation of the child or young person or of his labor."[51]

The Supplementary Convention proscribes the slave trade (Articles 3 and 4), and slavery itself and institutions similar to slavery, in Articles 5 and 6, thus putting into Convention form the principle laid down in article 4 of the Universal Declaration.

ii *Trafficking in Persons*

In 1949, immediately after the adoption of the Universal Declaration, the **Convention for the Suppression of the Traffic in Persons and the Exploitation of the Prostitution of Others** was adopted by General Assembly Resolution 317 (IV) on 2 December 1949.[52] This Convention followed the line of instruments adopted over the years on the "white slave traffic", some of them even before the creation of the League of Nations: the International Agreement of

50 Neither of these conventions is subject to direct supervision by the United Nations.

51 Supplementary Convention, Article 1.

52 Entered into force 25 July 1951.

18 May 1904 for the Suppression of the White Slave Traffic; the International Convention of 4 May 1910 for the Suppression of the White Slave Traffic; the International Convention of 30 September 1921 for the Suppression of the Traffic in Women and Children; and the International Convention of 11 October 1933 for the Suppression of the Traffic in Women of Full Age. (It is of course remarkable that these instruments focussed on slavery imposed on white women and children from developed countries.) The Preamble of the Convention notes that the League of Nations had already prepared a draft Convention in 1937 extending the scope of these instruments, and "developments since 1937 make feasible the conclusion of a convention consolidating the above-mentioned instruments and embodying the substance of the 1937 draft convention as well as desirable alterations therein".

The essence of the 1949 Convention is found in Article 1:

> *The Parties to the present Convention agree to punish any person who, to gratify the passions of another:*
> (*1*) *Procures, entices or leads away, for purposes of prostitution, another person, even with the consent of that person;*
> (*2*) *Exploits the prostitution of another person, even with the consent of that person.*

In 2000, the UN adopted the **Convention against Transnational Organized Crime (Palermo Convention)** and its supplementary **Protocol to Prevent, Suppress and Punish Trafficking in Persons, especially Women and Children**. It was intended to "prevent and combat trafficking in persons, to protect and assist victims of trafficking and to promote cooperation among States to achieve these objectives." This instrument took account of the fact that trafficking had become a much more widely practiced phenomenon in recent years, particularly with the end of the Communist system in Europe, the lowering of border restrictions and the easing of transport. The Protocol defines trafficking as follows:

> For the purposes of this Protocol:
> (a) "Trafficking in persons" shall mean the recruitment, transportation, transfer, harbouring or receipt of persons, by means of the threat or use of force or other forms of coercion, of abduction, of fraud, of deception, of the abuse of power or of a position of vulnerability or of the giving or receiving of payments or benefits to achieve the consent of a person having control over another person, for the purpose of exploitation. Exploitation shall include, at a minimum, the

> exploitation of the prostitution of others or other forms of sexual exploitation, forced labor or services, slavery or practices similar to slavery, servitude or the removal of organs.

This protocol has become the basic international document in this area.

iii *The Covenants*

The two International Covenants on human rights both include provisions relevant to this concern, in different degrees. *The International Covenant on Economic, Social and Cultural Rights* provides very little on it, its Article 6(1) echoing closely the provisions of the Universal Declaration:

> *The States Parties to the present Covenant recognise the right to work, which includes the opportunity of everyone to the opportunity to gain his living by work which he freely chooses or accepts, and will take appropriate steps to safeguard this right.*

The emphasis here is on the right to work and freedom of choice, not on the forced labor aspect of the problem.

The *International Covenant on Civil and Political Rights* contains a much fuller expression of this right in its Article 8, which is closer to the concept examined in this section of the present chapter:[53]

> 1. *No one shall be held in slavery; slavery and the slave-trade in all their forms shall be prohibited.*
> 2. *No one shall be held in servitude.*
> 3. (*a*) *No one shall be required to perform forced or compulsory labor;*
>   (*b*) *Paragraph 3 (a) shall not be held to preclude, in countries where imprisonment with hard labor may be imposed as a punishment for a crime, the performance of hard labor in pursuance of a sentence to such punishment by a competent court;*
>   (*c*) *For the purpose of this paragraph the term "forced or compulsory labor" shall not include:*
>   (*i*) *Any work or service, not referred to in subparagraph (b), normally required of a person who is under detention in conse-*

53 It is interesting that freedom from slavery was included as a civil-political right, and not as an economic or social right, when it is of course both. This is an illustration of the folly of separating these human rights into artificial categories.

quence of a lawful order of a court, or of a person during conditional release from such detention;

(*ii*) *Any service of a military character and, in countries where conscientious objection is recognized, any national service required by law of conscientious objectors;*

(*iii*) *Any service exacted in cases of emergency or calamity threatening the life or well-being of the community;*

(*iv*) *Any work or service which forms part of normal civil obligations.*

It will be seen below that this follows fairly closely the provisions of the ILO's Forced Labor Convention of 1930, and there does not appear to be any contradiction between them.

b International Labor Organization

Four years after the adoption of the Slavery Convention, the ILO adopted the *Forced Labor Convention, 1930 (No. 29)*, which focussed the prohibitions in the Slavery Convention as concerns international labor law, and provided for the regulations and exceptions that make it functional. Convention No. 29 is supervised vigorously by the ILO's supervisory bodies, and is considered one of the ILO's fundamental human rights instruments.

Under Article 1(1) of Convention No. 29, "Each Member ... which ratifies this Convention undertakes to suppress the use of forced or compulsory labor within the shortest possible period." This is moderated by paras. 2 and 3 of this Article, which allow for the use of this kind of labor during a "transitional period, for public purposes only and as an exceptional measure", but this transitional period was to be reconsidered by the Governing Body within 5 years. Articles 3 to 24 of the Convention provide various considerations for use during the transitional period; but the ILO's supervisory bodies now consider this period long past, and these provisions to be no longer in force.

The core of Convention No. 29 lies in its Article 2, which defines what kinds of forced labor are covered by the Convention; and also describes the kinds of labor that, while obligatory, cannot be considered to be prohibited forced labor:

1. *For the purposes of this Convention the term "forced or compulsory labor" shall mean all work or service which is exacted from any person under the menace of any penalty and for which the said person has not offered himself voluntarily.*
2. *Nevertheless, for the purposes of this Convention, the term "forced or compulsory labor" shall not include—*

(*a*) *any work or service exacted in virtue of compulsory military service laws for work of a purely military character;*
(*b*) *any work or service which forms part of the normal civic obligations of the citizens of a fully self-governing country;*
(*c*) *any work or service exacted from any person as a consequence of a conviction in a court of law, provided that the said work or service is carried out under the supervision and control of a public authority and that the said person is not hired to or placed at the disposal of private individuals, companies or associations;*
(*d*) *any work or service exacted in cases of emergency, that is to say, in the event of war or of a calamity or threatened calamity, such as fire, flood, famine, earthquake, violent epidemic or epizootic diseases, invasion by animal, insect or vegetable pests, and in general any circumstance that would endanger the existence or the well-being of the whole or part of the population;*
(*e*) *minor communal services of a kind which, being performed by the members of the community in the direct interest of the said community, can therefore be considered as normal civic obligations incumbent upon the members of the community, provided that the members of the community or their direct representatives shall have the right to be consulted in regard to the need for such services.*

Convention No. 29 concentrates in some respects on the use of forced or compulsory labor for private benefit, while the later Convention No. 105 (see below) emphasizes the aspect of forced labor as a government imposition. In addition to Art. 2(2)(c) quoted above, Article 4(1) provides that "The competent authority shall not impose or permit the imposition of forced or compulsory labor for the benefit of private individuals, companies or associations", and Article 5(1) states that "No concession granted to private individuals, companies or associations shall involve any form of forced or compulsory labor for the production or the collection of products which such private individuals, companies or associations utilise or in which they trade." As will be seen below, this focus on private benefit involves significant difficulties of interpretation in the context of the privatization of prisons and the increasing introduction of private companies into prison employment.[54]

54 It will be noted that Articles 3 to 24 of Convention No. 29 were intended to refer to colonial situations where forced labor had long been considered to be normal and even necessary, envisaged the gradual abolition of this kind of forced labor. These 'transitional' articles of the Convention are now considered to be out of date and are no longer in force.

The ILO supplemented the basic forced labor provisions with another instrument, the *Abolition of Forced Labor Convention, 1957* (*No. 105*), prohibiting the use of forced or compulsory labor for certain specified purposes. This Convention grew out of the abuses of labor committed by the Nazi regime in World War II, and by the Soviet Union in the punishment of political prisoners and other parts of the population. Article 1 provides:

> Each Member of the International Labor Organisation which ratifies this Convention undertakes to suppress and not to make use of any form of forced or compulsory labor:
> (*a*) *As a means of political coercion or education or as a punishment for holding or expressing political views or views ideologically opposed to the established political, social or economic system;*
> (*b*) *As a method of mobilising and using labor for purposes of economic development;*
> (*c*) *As a means of labor discipline;*
> (*d*) *As a punishment for having participated in strikes;*
> (*e*) *As a means of racial, social, national or religious discrimination.*

This Convention does not, as will be evident, address slavery or related institutions. It is instead dedicated to removing labor as an instrument of punishment, political repression and social control.

In early 2013 the ILO held an expert meeting[55] to discuss whether the existing provisions of the two Conventions outlined here needed to be supplemented. The Governing Body decided to put the item on the agenda of the 2014 International Labor Conference,[56] with a view to adopting standards for the following purpose:

> *The adoption of a new instrument or instruments supplementing the forced labor Conventions could therefore reinforce an integrated approach to prevention, victim protection and compensation and set out detailed provisions concerning the various measures to be taken in these three areas.*

---

55 See report of the meeting in ILO Governing Body document GB.317/INS/2 (Rev.), 317th Session of the Governing Body (March 2013), on the ILO web site.

56 The new standard(s) will be adopted in a single discussion procedure, which is sometimes used instead of the usual double discussion procedure when the aims of a particular standard-setting exercise are achievable in a singe discussion. The new standard(s) will therefore be adopted in June 2014, and will be available on the ILO web site.

c Regional Instruments

i *Europe*

The European Union Charter of Fundamental Rights provides in Article 5:

> **Prohibition of slavery and forced labor**
> 1. No one shall be held in slavery or servitude.
> 2. No one shall be required to perform forced or compulsory labor.
> 3. Trafficking in human beings is prohibited.

The European Convention on Human Rights develops these concepts in its Article 4, in terms that closely resemble ILO Convention No. 29:

> *Prohibition of slavery and forced labor*
> 4. No one shall be held in slavery or servitude.
> 5. No one shall be required to perform forced or compulsory labor.
> 6. For the purpose of this Article the term "forced or compulsory labor" shall not include:
>   (*a*) *any work required to be done in the ordinary course of detention imposed according to the provisions of Article 5 of this Convention or during conditional release from such detention;*
>   (*b*) *any service of a military character or, in case of conscientious objectors in countries where they are recognised, service exacted instead of compulsory military service;*
>   (*c*) *any service exacted in case of an emergency or calamity threatening the life or well-being of the community;*
>   (*d*) *any work or service which forms part of normal civic obligations.*

The European Court of Human Rights has issued a number of decisions on forced labor and trafficking, in application of the European Convention.[57] These cover a variety of issues, including forced labor of domestic workers, trafficking and forced prostitution, work during detention, military service and substitute service. The cases on forced labor of domestic workers has helped focus attention, inside and outside Europe, on the invisibility of these workers from national labor law and even criminal law, as they often are not covered by

57 See the Fact Sheet on Forced Labor and Trafficking, issued by the Press Unit of the Court, at http://www.echr.coe.int/Documents/FS_Forced_labor_ENG.pdf, which summarizes a number of cases. (Consulted 10 June 2013.)

labor codes and in far too many cases are not subject to labor inspection. See, for instance, the case of **Siliadin v. France** (2005), in which a Togolese national having arrived in France in 1994 with the intention to study, was made to work instead as a domestic servant in a private household in Paris. Her passport confiscated, she worked without pay, 15 hours a day, without a day off, for several years. The applicant complained about having been a domestic slave. The European Court of Human Rights found that the applicant had not been enslaved because her employers, although exercising control over her, had not had "a genuine right of legal ownership over her reducing her to the status of an "object". It held, however, that the criminal law in force at the time had not protected her sufficiently, and that although the law had been changed subsequently, it had not been applicable to her situation. The Court concluded that the applicant had been held in servitude, in **violation of Article 4** (prohibition of slavery, servitude, forced or compulsory labor) of the European Convention on Human Rights.

The large number of such cases on trafficking, for either labor exploitation or sexual exploitation, also illustrates how prevalent these practices are even in countries with a relatively pervasive legal culture and law enforcement. It is striking that most of the cases mentioned in the European Court's summary of cases listed in the Fact Sheet already cited, have either been declared inadmissible or have been dismissed for one reason or another, illustrating how seldom trafficking is effectively prosecuted anywhere in the world.

ii *The Americas*

The *American Declaration of the Rights and Duties of Man*, adopted a few months before the Universal Declaration, contains no general statement of freedom from forced labor, though it does proclaim in its Article 1 the "right to life, liberty and the security of the person", which may be held to encompass this principle.

The 1969 *American Convention on Human Rights*, in its Article 6, prohibits slavery and forced labor in detail, in terms closely resembling ILO Convention No. 29 and the European Convention.

1. *No one shall be subject to slavery or to involuntary servitude, which are prohibited in all their forms, as are the slave trade and traffic in women.*
2. *No one shall be required to perform forced or compulsory labor. This provision shall not be interpreted to mean that, in those countries in which the penalty established for certain crimes is deprivation of*

liberty at forced labor, the carrying out of such a sentence imposed by a competent court is prohibited. Forced labor shall not adversely affect the dignity or the physical or intellectual capacity of the prisoner.

3. *For the purposes of this article, the following do not constitute forced or compulsory labor:*
   (*a*) *any work or service normally required of a person imprisoned in execution of a sentence or formal decision passed by the competent judicial authority. Such work or service shall be carried out under the supervision and control of public authorities, and any persons performing such work or service shall not be placed at the disposal of any private party, company, or judicial person;*
   (*b*) *any military service and, in countries in which conscientious objectors are recognized, national service that the law may provide for in lieu of that service;*
   (*c*) *any service exacted in time of danger or calamity that threatens the existence or well-being of the community; or*
   (*d*) *any work or service that forms part of normal civic obligations.*

The *Additional Protocol* to the American Convention on Human Rights in the Area of Economic, Social and Cultural Rights, contains no additional provisions on freedom from forced labor.

iii *Africa*

The *African Charter on Human and Peoples' Rights* contains only one brief provision on this subject, at Article 5:

> *Every individual shall have the right to the respect of the dignity inherent in a human being and to the recognition of his legal status. All forms of exploitation and degradation of man particularly slavery, slave trade, torture, cruel, inhuman or degrading punishment and treatment shall be prohibited.*

iv *Asia*

The 2012 ASEAN Declaration on Human Rights contains the following provision:

> 13. *No person shall be held in servitude or slavery in any of its forms, or be subject to human smuggling or trafficking in persons, including for the purpose of trafficking in human organs.*

d International Supervision

There are three principal sources for examining the actual practice of forced and compulsory labor and slavery today. The ILO Committee of Experts carries out the most systematic and detailed examination covering more than 170 countries that have ratified one or both of the two ILO Conventions on the subject. At the United Nations, the Human Rights Committee and the Committee on Economic, Social and Cultural Rights also examine governments' reports, on a smaller sample each year but covering as large a number of countries over time. Finally, the United Nations Human Rights Council includes freedom from forced labor and slavery in its examination of national human rights performance under the Universal Periodic Review mechanism.

The predecessor to the Human Rights Council, the Commission on Human Rights, had various subsidiary bodies that are no longer in existence, though many of them did very useful work. The now-defunct Working Group on Contemporary Forms of Slavery (WGCS) examined situations each year in which both general concerns and allegations about specific countries—mostly from non-governmental organizations—were aired. It is worth beginning with one of the conclusions of the WGCS at its 1997 session:

> A review of the information provided to the Working Group showed that despite the progress made in the protection of human rights and the preservation of human dignity all over the world, various forms of slavery still existed and new insidious forms of slavery were emerging. The Working Group considered in particular the questions of child and bonded labor, sexual exploitation, especially of children, the traffic in persons, migrant and domestic workers, (and) sexual violence during wartime.[58]

This is a good statement of the range of problems that can still be discerned in examining these supervisory bodies' conclusions, and illustrates that the resurgence of this kind of slavery has been going on for some time.

i *The ILO*

Among the reports issued on fundamental human rights issues by the ILO are annual Global Reports, initially issued to follow up the 1998 Declaration of

---

58 Report of the Working Group on Contemporary Forms of Slavery, 1997, UN Doc. E/CN.4/Sub.2/1997/13.

Fundamental Principles and Rights at Work. The 2009 Global Report[59] was on forced labor, and it quoted the figures published in another such report 4 years earlier. It stated that detailed statistics gathered by the ILO

> ... show the truly global scope of the problem, which affects virtually all countries and all kinds of economies. Some 12.3 million persons worldwide were in some form of forced labor or bondage. Of these, 9.8 million were exploited by private agents, including more than 2.4 million in forced labor as a result of human trafficking. The highest numbers have been found in Asia, some 9.4 million, followed by approximately 1.3 million in Latin America and the Caribbean, and at least 360,000 in the industrialized countries. Some 56 per cent of all persons in forced labor were women and girls. The annual profits, from human trafficking alone, were at least US$32 billion.

The 2009 Global Report found that it was too soon to repeat the detailed statistical analysis that had yielded these figures in 2005, though it increased the estimate of the number or peoples in forced labor to nearly 21 million. It did add, however, that the ILO estimated

> ... that the "opportunity cost" of coercion to the workers affected by these abusive practices, in terms of lost earnings, now reaches over US$20 billion. This presents a powerful economic argument, as well as a moral imperative, as to why governments must now accord higher priority to these concerns.

The ILO Committee of Experts examines the application of Conventions Nos. 29 and 105, which have been ratified by 177 and 174 countries respectively (as of November 2013). The Committee's General Surveys cover this question as well, with the most recentbeing the 2007 Survey on The Eradication of Forced Labor, and a somewhat briefer Survey in 2012 on the Fundamental Conventions.[60] Forced labor questions are also examined under the Worst Forms of Child Labor Convention, 1999 (No. 182), the Indigenous and Tribal Peoples Convention, 1989 (No. 169) and others. A certain number of problems arise most frequently.

---

59 *The cost of coercion.* Report of the Director-General, Global Report under the follow-up to the ILO Declaration on Fundamental Principles and Rights at Work, International Labor Conference, 98th Session 2009, Report I(B), pp. 1 and 2.

60 See the compilation of General Surveys on the ILO web site, under NORMLEX.

a. **Traditional slavery and forced labor.** In a small number of countries, there are serious allegations that traditional slavery and large-scale forced labor, and in some cases these allegations have been heavily substantiated. This tends to be practiced against vulnerable groups such as indigenous and tribal peoples or other minority populations. See, for example, the following extract from an observation by the Committee of Experts in 2011:

> Articles 1(1), 2(1) and 25 of the Convention. "*Slave labor*". In the comments it has been addressing to the Government for a number of years on the issue of "slave labor", the Committee has noted several measures which have been taken by the Government in order to reinforce its legislative and institutional framework to combat this practice, under which many workers continue to be victims of inhuman and degrading conditions, debt bondage or internal trafficking for purposes of labor exploitation. The Committee emphasized, in particular, the adaptation of the legislation to national circumstances through section 149 of the Penal Code, which defines the elements that constitute the crime of "reducing a person to a condition akin to that of slavery"; the activities undertaken by specialized institutions to combat this phenomenon, such as the National Commission to Eradicate Slave Labor and the Special Mobile Inspection Group; and the action of Labor Courts, which have sanctioned persons engaged in these forms of exploitation with fines and have provided for substantial compensation. Noting that all of these actions have failed to be sufficiently dissuasive to prevent certain employers from having recourse to this practice, which remains lucrative, the Committee requested the Government to continue taking action without respite against persons who exact forced labor by adopting measures in the fields of legislation, labor inspection and the judicial authorities. The Committee notes that, following her visit to the country, the United Nations Special Rapporteur on contemporary forms of slavery, including its causes and consequences, addressed recommendations to the Government that are consistent with those made by the Committee in its observations (A/HRC/15/20/Add.4).[61]

---

61 Observation concerning the application of Convention No. 29 by Brazil, adopted 2011, Report of the Committee of Experts on the Application of Conventions and Recommendations, submitted to the International Labor Conference in June 2012.

b. **Trafficking in persons.** Trafficking is considered to be covered by Convention No. 29 as one aspect of forced labor, as well as by the Worst Forms of Child Labor Convention, 1999 (No. 182). The Committee of Experts refers to it regularly, for example in the following extract of a comment adopted by the Committee at its 2012 session. This observation also illustrates that the supervisory bodies of the ILO and the United Nations take careful account of each others' examinations of national situations:

> The Committee notes that the Committee on Economic, Social and Cultural Rights, in its concluding observations of 12 June 2009, expressed serious concern regarding reports that an estimated 400–800 Cambodian women and children are trafficked to foreign countries per month, as well as regarding the low number of prosecutions and convictions of traffickers (E/C.12/KHM/CO/1, paragraph 26). The Committee further notes that the Committee against Torture, in its concluding observations of 20 January 2011, expressed concern regarding reports that a high number of women and children continue to be trafficked from, through and within the country for purposes of sexual exploitation and forced labor (CAT/C/KHM/CO/2, paragraph 22). ***The Committee urges the Government to strengthen its efforts to combat trafficking in persons, including within the framework of the national action plan 2011–13 on the suppression of human trafficking and sexual exploitation, and to provide information on the measures taken in this regard. It requests the Government to provide information, in its next report, on the application of the Law on Suppression of Human Trafficking and Sexual Exploitation (2008) in practice, including the number of investigations, prosecutions, convictions and specific penalties imposed. It further requests the Government to indicate the measures taken to provide training to law enforcement officials, including labor inspectors, on the phenomenon of trafficking. Lastly, the Committee requests the Government to supply information on the specific measures taken to provide protection and assistance to victims of trafficking, as well as the results achieved.***[62]

c. **Bonded labor.** This is also known as *debt bondage*, and is theoretically different from slavery because it is imposed only during the period required to repay a debt incurred. In practice, there is no real difference, because abuses

62 Observation concerning the application of Convention No. 29 by Cambodia, adopted 2012, Report of the Committee of Experts on the Application of Conventions and Recommendations, submitted to the International Labor Conference in June 2013.

often make it virtually impossible ever to discharge the debt. It is in fact often passed on between generations, with some people giving their children into bondage to repay their debts. This phenomenon is best known in *India* and in other countries of the Indian sub-continent, but may be found elsewhere on occasion. The following extract from an observation made by the Committee of Experts in 2012 reflects a long series of such comments made over the years, showing only gradual response by India to international pressure:

> Articles 1(1), 2(1) and 25 of the Convention. Bonded labor. Magnitude of the problem. The Committee refers to its earlier comments in which it noted the allegations made by the International Trade Union Confederation (ITUC), based on findings from various research studies, that bonded labor in agriculture and in industries like mining, brick kilns, silk and cotton production, and bidi making was likely to be affecting millions of workers across the country. The Committee asked the Government on numerous occasions to undertake a national survey on bonded labor, with the involvement of the social partners and using any statistical methods it considers appropriate.
>
> The Committee takes due note of the Government's views expressed in its report that such a national survey cannot be done by using statistical tools/methodologies adopted for the purpose of collecting data on any issue on a macro basis. The Government considers that the issues relating to the identification of bonded labor are sensitive in nature, which requires that the interviewers have to collect information by interviewing the affected persons about the nature of exploitation and their service conditions, in order to be able to identify whether they fall in the category of bonded labor. The Government reiterates that it had provided grants to state governments for conducting district-level surveys of bonded labor, and that a large number of such surveys had been conducted by the state governments. In this regard, the Committee previously noted a detailed report on the survey conducted in the State of Gujarat, supplied by the Government. On the other hand, the Committee noted that the Government, in cooperation with the ILO, was about to undertake a detailed survey on the vulnerable groups of workers who often become victims of bonded labor.
>
> ***While taking due note of the above information, the Committee trusts that the Government will see no difficulty in preparing a nationwide survey on bonded labor, in cooperation with the ILO and with the involvement of the social partners, by compiling the existing data from all the district-level surveys referred to above conducted by all state***

> ***governments and using any statistical methodology that might be considered appropriate. The Committee hopes that the Government will soon be in a position to provide information on the progress made in this regard.***[63]

d. **Use of forced labor for development.** This arises under both ILO Conventions (Nos. 29 and 105), which approach the problem from different angles—C. 29 exempts from its coverage forced labor for compulsory military service, but not for compulsory development work even when carried out by conscripts, while C. 105 prohibits forced labor as a means of national development. The result is often the same. The following extract of a comment on Convention No. 105 illustrates that while this practice has been abandoned in most countries, the national legislation has not always kept pace with practice:

> Article 1(b) and (c). Imposition of prison sentences involving an obligation to work for the purposes of economic development and as a means of labor discipline. For many years, the Committee has been emphasizing the need to amend or repeal certain provisions of Act No. 5/82 of 9 June 1989 concerning the defence of the economy. This Act provides for the punishment of conduct which, directly or indirectly, jeopardizes economic development, prevents the implementation of the State National Plan or is detrimental to the material or spiritual well-being of the population. Sections 10, 12, 13 and 14 of the Act prescribe prison sentences involving compulsory labor in repeated cases of failure to fulfil the economic obligations set forth in instructions, directives, procedures, etc., governing the preparation or implementation of the State National Plan. Section 7 of the Act penalizes unintentional conduct (such as negligence, the lack of a sense of responsibility, etc.) resulting in the infringement of managerial or disciplinary standards.
>
> The Government previously indicated that Act No. 5/82 concerning the defence of the economy and Act No. 9/87 amending it were repealed by the Assembly of the Republic on 21 March 2007. The Committee noted, however, that on 20 June 2007 the Constitutional Council declared the law adopted by the Assembly repealing Acts Nos. 5/82 and 9/87 to be unconstitutional, considering that the blanket repeal of these Acts would

63 Observation concerning the application of Convention No. 29 by India, adopted 2012, Report of the Committee of Experts on the Application of Conventions and Recommendations, submitted to the International Labor Conference in June 2013.

have the effect of no longer criminalizing or punishing certain conducts that jeopardize economic development which are not punishable by other legislative texts, thereby leaving a legal vacuum. ***Noting that the Government has not supplied any information in its latest report on the current status of Act No. 5/82 concerning the defence of the economy and Act No. 9/87 amending it, the Committee invites the Government to pursue its efforts to decriminalize the conducts and breaches provided for in the abovementioned provisions of Act No. 9/82 and Act No. 9/87 and to take the necessary steps, in the context of the reform of the penal legislation, to repeal the provisions of Act No. 5/82, as amended by Act No. 9/87, which are contrary to the Convention.***[64]

e. **Prison labor.** Special mention should be made of the question of prison labor, especially for private undertakings. The Committee of Experts carried out a special survey of developments on this question in its 1997 report,[65] and returned to the subject in its General Survey of 2007.[66] Convention No. 29 exempted "*any work or service exacted from any person as a consequence of a conviction in a court of law, provided that the said work or service is carried out under the supervision and control of a public authority and that the said person is not hired to or placed at the disposal of private individuals, companies or associations*" (Art. 2(2)(c)). This provision is apparently simple, and until fairly recently caused few problems of interpretation. However, there has been an explosive growth in the use of prison labor for private purposes, in two respects. An increasing number of private companies are setting up workshops or other workplaces inside prisons, while in some cases prisons are being run as private undertakings. The major questions that arise are the following.

Consent. The Convention prohibits prisoners being "hired to or placed at the disposal of" private interests. The Committee has considered that this necessarily implies that the prisoner's consent is required before working in this way. As indicated by the Committee of Experts in 1997, this consent is required only for work for private individuals or enterprises: "The Convention does not require that they (prisoners) should have a choice as to whether to work in

64 Observation concerning the application of Convention No. 105 by Mozambique, adopted 2012, Report of the Committee of Experts on the Application of Conventions and Recommendations, submitted to the International Labor Conference in June 2013.

65 Report of the Committee of Experts, 1997, Report III(1A), 86th ILC (1998), paras. 95 to 125.

66 Report III (Part 1B), International Labor Conference, 96th Session, 2007.

prison—it explicitly allows the imposition of labor in prison, under the conditions laid down."[67]

Supervision. There are also problems with privatised prisons, of whether the work is carried out *under the supervision and control of a public authority* as required in the Convention. This is particularly difficult with privately operated prisons, which may imply that foremen for private companies make decisions on work performance that might have an effect on release on parole. As the Committee of Experts stated in its 1997 review of the situation, "No general prescription may be laid down which will cover all the possible arrangements for this. The Committee considers, however, that if the supervision and control are restricted to a general authority to inspect the premises periodically, this by itself would not appear to meet the requirement of the Convention for supervision and control."[68]

There follows an extract from an observation made by the Committee of Experts in 2012 that illustrates the questions raised, as well as the fact that some countries seem to moving away from such practices:

> Articles 1(1), 2(1) and 2(2)(c) of the Convention. Work of prisoners for private enterprises. In comments made for a number of years, the Committee referred to the situation of prisoners in the country who, in law and practice, are obliged to work, without their consent, in workshops run by private enterprises within state prisons, in conditions not comparable to those found in the free labor market. The Committee recalled that work by prisoners for private enterprises can be held compatible with the Convention only where the necessary safeguards exist to ensure that the prisoners concerned offer themselves voluntarily, without being subjected to pressure or the menace of any penalty, by giving their formal, free and informed consent to work for private enterprises. In such a situation, work of prisoners for private parties would not come under the scope of the Convention, since no compulsion is involved. Moreover, the Committee has considered that, in the prison context, the most reliable indicator of the voluntariness of labor is that the work is performed under conditions which approximate a free labor relationship, including wages, social security and occupational safety and health. In this connection, the Committee previously noted that the requirement of the prisoner's formal consent to be employed in a workshop run by a private enterprise, laid down in section 41(3) of the Act on the execution of

67 Report of the Committee of Experts, 1997, op. cit., para. 120.

68 Ibid., para. 124.

sentences of 1976, had been suspended by the Second Act to improve the budget structure, of 22 December 1981. It therefore requested that measures be taken to ensure that formal, free and informed consent is required for the work of prisoners in private enterprise workshops inside prison premises.

The Committee notes the information in the Government's report that in September 2011, ten federal states (Länder) (Brandenburg, Berlin, Bremen, Mecklenburg-Western Pomerania, Rhineland-Palatinate, Schleswig-Holstein, Saarland, Saxony and Thuringia) presented a common model Penal Enforcement Bill, and that this model does not require a prisoner to work. The Committee welcomes this initiative and notes that section 22(1) of the model Penal Enforcement Bill states that work shall be assigned to prisoners upon their request or with their consent.[69]

f. **Labor discipline.** It may seem strange that one of the problems arising under the forced labor Conventions in the ILO is conditions of work for merchant seafarers, in particular penalizing seafarers because they do not take orders that other workers would not be required to take.[70] In a number of countries, merchant seafarers are still covered by older legislation which has not been adapted to them as workers, but which still imposes the harsh discipline of another century. Two problems arise most frequently: merchant seafarers may be "forcibly conveyed" back on ship if they decide to resign their jobs without permission in a port away from the home countries—i.e., treated as deserters rather than as workers who wish to resign—or any failure to perform their jobs properly (or at least to the captain's satisfaction) makes them subject to prosecution for criminal offenses, often involving prison sentences with compulsory labor. The following 2012 observation illustrates how this is dealt with.

Article 1(c) of the Convention. Imposition of forced labor as a means of labor discipline. In reply to the Committee's comments on the need to amend certain provisions of the Merchant Shipping Penal and

69 Observation concerning the application of Convention No. 29 by Germany, adopted 2012, Report of the Committee of Experts on the Application of Conventions and Recommendations, submitted to the International Labor Conference in June 2013.

70 It may be noted that there are a number of ILO Conventions dealing specifically with the conditions of work of merchant seafarers, most comprehensively the Maritime Labor Convention, 2006.

Disciplinary Code, 1943, which are not in conformity with the Convention, the Government once again indicates that the revision of this Code is under way, now within the framework of the Committee set up within the Ministry of Justice which is working on a revision of the Code.

The Committee recalls that, under section 132 of the Merchant Shipping Penal and Disciplinary Code, a crew member who deserts at the port of embarkation is liable to a prison sentence of up to one year, while desertion in any other port may be punished by a sentence of two years. Under section 137, a crew member who fails to carry out orders issued by his superiors in relation to services which do not endanger the safety of the vessel may be punished by a prison sentence of one to six months. A crew member who refuses to obey an order and subsequently carries it out voluntarily may be punished by a maximum of three months' imprisonment. These provisions are contrary to the Convention in so far as they allow prison sentences to be imposed (involving compulsory labor under sections 13 and 50(c) of the Prison Regulations of 9 July 1981) for certain breaches of labor discipline which do not endanger the safety of the vessel or the life or health of persons on board.

The Committee trusts that the process of revision of the Merchant Shipping Penal and Disciplinary Code will be completed in the near future in order to ensure that breaches of labor discipline which do not endanger the safety of the vessel or the life or health of persons on board are not punishable with a prison sentence. Please provide a copy of the new Code once adopted.[71]

g. **Political opinion.** Convention No. 105 bans the use of forced or compulsory labor to punish a range of offenses, including the expression of political opinion. There is no country that makes a direct link between political opinion and compulsory labor. The problem arises when political offenses are considered as ordinary crimes, and all those convicted of criminal offenses are subject to compulsory labor while in prison. In such cases, the Committee of Experts points out that imprisonment with forced labor for such offenses is incompatible with the Convention, and that the government should either stop punishing people for such offenses or modify the punishment to which they are

71 Observation concerning the application of Convention No. 105 by Angola, adopted 2012, Report of the Committee of Experts on the Application of Conventions and Recommendations, submitted to the International Labor Conference in June 2013.

subject. The following extract of a Committee of Experts comment illustrates the way in which the ILO has handled this question:

> The Committee takes notes of the following provisions of the Penal Code, the application of which could affect compliance with the Convention:
> - sections 136 and 137: insulting members of the National Assembly, the Government and depositories of authority conferred for the purpose of law enforcement;
> - section 155bis: the wearing in public of the uniform, insignia or emblem of an association or de facto group dissolved by the competent public authority;
> - section 209: the circulation of tracts, bulletins or flyers of foreign origin or inspiration of a nature such as to harm the national interest, and section 211(3): the displaying in public places of drawings, posters, engravings, paintings, photographs or any object or image of a nature likely to cause a breach of the peace.
>
> The Committee also notes Legislative Ordinance No. 25-557 on penalties for contravention of measures of a general nature, Legislative Ordinances Nos. 300 and 301 on the punishment of offences against the Head of State and foreign Heads of State, and the Legislative Decree of 14 January 1961 on subversive propaganda.
>
> The Committee notes that breach of the abovementioned provisions is punishable by penal servitude and that persons sentenced to penal servitude are employed either in or outside the prison in work authorized by the regulations of the establishment or determined by the President of the Republic (section 8 of the Penal Code).
>
> ***The Committee points out that observance of the Convention may be affected by the imposition of penal servitude on persons expressing certain political opinions. It requests the Government to provide information on the application of the abovementioned provisions in practice, particularly the number of sentences passed, and to provide copies of the relevant judicial decisions.***[72]

h. **Strikes or other action.** The last of the major problems that arise under Convention No. 105 is the punishment with forced labor for participating

72 Observation concerning the application of Convention No. 105 by the Democratic Republic of Congo, adopted 2012, Report of the Committee of Experts on the Application of Conventions and Recommendations, submitted to the International Labor Conference in June 2013.

in unauthorized strikes. This ties in with the treatment of this question by the ILO under Conventions Nos. 87 and 98 on freedom of association, and by the UN Committee on Economic, Social and Cultural Rights, dealt with below. The following extract from a Committee of Experts comment illustrates how this is dealt with.

> *Article 1(d). Penal sanctions involving compulsory labor as a punishment for having participated in strikes.* In its earlier comments, the Committee referred to certain provisions of the Labor Act punishing persons engaged in an unlawful collective action with sanctions of imprisonment, which involves compulsory prison labor.... The Committee noted, in particular, that section 104(2), and (3) of the Labor Act, as amended, not only prohibits collective job action in essential services and in the case of the agreement of the parties to refer the dispute to arbitration, but also provides for other restrictions on the right to collective job action related to procedural requirements, which are equally enforceable with sanctions of imprisonment (involving compulsory prison labor), under sections 109(1), (2) and 112(1) of the Act. Besides, it follows from the wording of section 102(b) of the Act that the Minister can declare as essential any service, other than that interruption of which would endanger the life, personal safety or health of the whole or part of the population. The Committee recalled that *Article 1(d)* of the Convention prohibits the use of forced or compulsory labor as a punishment for having participated in strikes.
>
> The Committee notes the Government's statement in its report that these sections of the Labor Act are included in the draft Principles for the Harmonization and Review of Labor Laws in Zimbabwe, which are currently being finalized by the social partners and will be submitted to the ILO following Cabinet approval. In August 2011, the social partners agreed to the principle of streamlining mechanisms to deal with collective job action and review ministerial powers and those of the Labor Court on collective job action. This principle would provide the framework to amend section 103 defining essential services, section 104 on balloting for strike action, sections 107, 109 and 112 on excessive penalties, including lengthy periods of imprisonment and de-registration of trade unions and dismissal of employees involved in collective job action.
>
> ***In these circumstances, the Committee trusts that the necessary measures will soon be taken to amend the provisions of the Labor Act imposing restrictions on the right to strike enforceable with sanctions involving compulsory prison labor, so as to ensure that no such sanctions can be imposed for the mere fact of organizing or peacefully participating in***

> ***strikes. The Committee requests the Government to provide, in its next report, information on the progress made in this regard.***[73]

ii *The United Nations*

Examination by the United Nations' treaty bodies of problems relating to forced labor is, by comparison, considerably more limited though nevertheless increasing in frequency. The *Human Rights Committee*, examining the application of the International Covenant on Civil and Political Rights, has been raising this question in relation to trafficking in persons since this became a more generalized phenomenon. See the following extract of a concluding observation, for instance:

> 13. While noting the various measures taken by the State party to combat trafficking in persons, in particular for sexual exploitation and forced labor purposes, the Committee is concerned about the persistence of such a phenomenon in the State party (art. 8).
>
> The State party should systematically and vigorously investigate allegations of trafficking in persons, prosecute and, if convicted, punish those responsible and provide compensation. The State party should also strengthen its support and protection measures at the Federal and Länder levels to victims and witnesses, including rehabilitation. It should further facilitate access to justice for victims of trafficking without fear of retaliation and regularly evaluate the impact of all initiatives and measures taken to counter trafficking in persons.[74]

Another instance of a concluding observation on this issue is the following:

> 18. The Committee is concerned at reports of continued cases of trafficking in persons, which mainly affect women and children (arts. 3, 8 and 24).
>
> The State party should take all necessary measures to ensure that victims of trafficking in persons are provided with medical, psychological, social and legal assistance. Protection should be provided to all witnesses and

---

73 Observation concerning the application of Convention No. 105 by Zimbabwe, adopted 2012, Report of the Committee of Experts on the Application of Conventions and Recommendations, submitted to the International Labor Conference in June 2013.

74 Human Rights Committee, Concluding observations on the sixth periodic report of Germany, adopted by the Committee at its 106th session (15 October–2 November 2012), UN doc. CCPR/C/DEU/CO/6.

> victims of trafficking so that they may have a place of refuge and an opportunity to give evidence against those held responsible. The State party should also continue to reinforce international cooperation as well as existing measures to combat trafficking in persons and the demand for trafficking. It should also devout (sic) sufficient resources to investigations of cases of trafficking in persons by identifying those responsible, prosecuting them and imposing penalties that are commensurate with the seriousness of the acts committed.[75]

The Human Rights Committee has also raised the forced recruitment of child soldiers, as in the following extract of a concluding observation:

> 17. While noting efforts by the State party to eradicate the practice of forced recruitment of child soldiers, including the establishment of disarmament, demobilization and reintegration commissions, and the reference made by the State party to the disarmament, demobilization and reintegration commission web site, the Committee remains concerned at the small number of children who have actually been demobilized. It also notes the statement by the State party that in the absence of a comprehensive civil register it is difficult to determine the exact ages of the people serving in its armed forces. (arts. 8 and 24 of the Covenant)
>
> The State party should put an end to all recruitment and use of child soldiers, and provide disarmament, demobilization and reintegration commissions with the human and financial resources they need to fulfill their mandates, in order to ensure the expertise required to demobilize child soldiers. The State party should also speed up its programme for the establishment of a civil register, and ensure that all births are registered throughout the country.[76]

In situations such as the one discussed in the concluding observation cited above, issues involving abduction and forced labor also arise. The same concluding observation included the following:

75 Human Rights Committee, Concluding observations on the fourth periodic report of the Philippines, adopted by the Committee at its 106th session (15 October–2 November 2012), UN doc. CPR/C/PHL/CO/4.

76 Concluding observations of the Human Rights Committee concerning the Sudan, 29 August 2007, CCPR/C/SDN/CO/3.

> 18. While noting efforts by the State party to eradicate the practice of abducting women and children and secure the return of abductees, in the light of reports from non-governmental sources and the State party of large numbers of abductions the Committee remains concerned at the small numbers of people who are traced. The Committee also takes note of the explanations put forward regarding the role and responsibility of tribes in the matter. (arts. 8 and 24 of the Covenant)
>
> The State party should put a stop to all forms of slavery and abduction in its territory and prosecute those engaging in such practices. It should make available to the Committee for the Elimination of Abduction of Women and Children the human and financial resources it needs to fulfill its mandate. The State party should also provide abductees with assistance in settling back into their families and communities. It enjoins the State party to hold the tribes more accountable, and to take forceful action against tribes that continue to engage in abduction.[77]

A pressing issue for a few countries, especially in the Indian subcontinent, is debt bondage. As concerns *India*, the Committee's last examination of a report (as of the time of publication)[78] was in 1997, when it included the following in its concluding observation:

> 29. The Committee expresses concern at the extent of bonded labor, as well as the fact that the incidence of this practice reported to the Supreme Court is far higher than is mentioned in the report. The Committee also notes with concern that eradication measures which have been taken do not appear to be effective in achieving real progress in the release and rehabilitation of bonded laborers. Therefore:
>
> the Committee recommends that a thorough study be urgently undertaken to identify the extent of bonded labor and that more effective measures be taken to eradicate this practice, in accordance with the Bonded Labor System (Abolition) Act of 1976 and article 8 of the Covenant.[79]

---

77 Ibid.

78 By mid-2013, the periodic report of India due at the end of 2001 had not been received.

79 Concluding observations of the Human Rights Committee on India, 08/04/1997, CCPR/C/79/Add.81. The ILO has also been requesting a comprehensive study of debt bondage, which the Government has failed to implement—see above.

The *Committee on Economic, Social and Cultural Rights* also examines this question. That Committee has referred to forced labor imposed as a punishment for persons found guilty of crimes (reflecting ILO Convention No. 105), as being in violation of Articles 6 and 7 of the Covenant. The following extract of a concluding observation illustrates this point:

> The Committee is concerned about the use of forced labor as a corrective measure or as a penal sanction against persons found guilty of a crime, as provided for in the Penal Code and Labor Code, in particular article 35 of the Constitution and article 95.6 of the Penalty Execution Code in which prisoners are prohibited to stop their labor activity and go on strike. (arts. 6 and 7)
>
> **The Committee recommends that the State party abolish the use of forced labor either as a corrective measure or as a penal sentence against persons found guilty of a crime and amend or repeal the relevant provision of the Penal Code and the Labor Code, in accordance with article 6 of the Covenant.**[80]

This Committee, like other UN system supervisory bodies, has also made comments on the effects of human trafficking on the enjoyment of the Covenant's protection of human rights. See, for instance, the following extract from the report of a 2011 examination of a national report:

> 17. The Committee is concerned about human trafficking in the State party and regrets the inadequacy of Act No. 26364 on the matter. It is also concerned by the insufficiency of measures for the rehabilitation of victims of trafficking and exploitation (art. 10, para. 3).
>
> **The Committee recommends that the State party accelerate the process of revising its legislation on combatting human trafficking to international standards. It also recommends that the State party increase the resource allocations for the prevention of human trafficking, the prosecution and conviction of perpetrators, and the provision of support to victims, as well as for enhancing coordination among all levels in this respect.**[81]

---

80 Committee on Economic, Social and Cultural Rights, Concluding observations on the third periodic report of Azerbaijan, adopted by the Committee at its fiftieth session (29 April–17 May 2013) (ADVANCED UNEDITED VERSION).

81 Concluding observations of the Committee on Economic, Social and Cultural Rights on Argentina, Forty-seventh session, (14 November–2 December 2011), UN doc. E/C.12/ARG/CO/3.

In addition, the Committee on Economic, Social and Cultural Rights refers to bonded labor, though in a different way from the Human Rights Committee, as in the following extract from a concluding observation:

> 18. The Committee is concerned that, in spite of the abolition in 2002 of the system of bonded labor, there are still significant difficulties faced by the freed bonded laborers regarding their access to work and livelihood and appropriate education for their children. The Committee is also concerned that the lack of employment opportunities in the State party hinders the advancement from feudal relations to relations based on equality, particularly for ex-Kamaiyas and ex-Haliyas, many of whom have returned to the same condition of bonded labor from which they were supposedly freed.[82]

2 *The Right to Freedom of Choice of Work*

Freedom of choice has both legal and practical implications. As indicated in the previous section, there have been cases in which governments have restricted the choice of individuals by assigning work to them, so that they are subject to penalties if they do not perform the work assigned. For this reason, the ILO's Employment Policy Convention, 1964 (No. 122) consecrates the principle of "full, productive and freely-chosen employment" as an obligation on ratifying countries.

Another factor is that governments are required under several international Conventions, not to mention good practice, to provide services whereby potential employees can be put in touch with potential employers. Placement services are available in almost all countries, though they are often limited in scope and function more or less well. The international standards governing this are the ILO's Employment Service Convention, 1948 (No. 88), and the Fee-Charging Employment Agencies Convention (Revised), 1949 (No. 96). The most recent Convention adopted on this subject is the Private Employment Agencies Convention, 1997 (No. 181).

Over the years the ILO supervisory bodies have questioned the obligation to perform either military or civil service that does not fall within the exemptions from the definition of forced labor found in Article 2 of Convention No. 29. While this is a less prevalent question than in earlier years, it still arises. See for instance the following extract from an observation by the ILO Committee of Experts:

---

82 Concluding observations of the Committee on Economic, Social and Cultural Rights on Nepal, Thirty-eighth session (30 April–18 May 2007), UN doc. E/C.12/NPL/CO/2.

> Article 2(1) of the Convention. Civil service. For a number of years the Committee has been drawing the Government's attention to the incompatibility with the Convention of sections 32, 33, 34 and 38 of Act No. 84–10 of 11 February 1984 concerning civil service, as amended and supplemented by Act No. 86–11 of 19 August 1986 and by Act No. 06–15 of 14 November 2006, under which it is possible to require persons who have completed a course of higher education or training to perform a period of civil service ranging from one to four years before being able to exercise an occupation or obtain employment.
>
> The Committee also previously noted that, under sections 32 and 38 of the Act, any refusal to perform civil service and the resignation of the person concerned without valid reason results in the prohibition on their exercising an activity on their own account, and that any infringement will incur the penalties laid down in section 243 of the Penal Code (imprisonment ranging from three months to two years and/or a fine of between 500 and 5,000 dinars). Similarly, under sections 33 and 34 of the Act, all private employers are required to satisfy themselves before engaging any workers that applicants are not subject to civil service or can produce documentation proving that they have completed it. Furthermore, any private employer who knowingly employs a citizen who has evaded civil service is liable to imprisonment and a fine. Hence, even though persons liable to civil service enjoy conditions of work (remuneration, seniority, promotion, retirement, etc.) similar to those of regular public sector workers, they perform this service under threat since, in the event of any refusal, they are denied access to any self-employed occupational activity or employment in the private sector. This means that civil service falls within the concept of compulsory labor within the meaning of *Article 2(1)* of the Convention. Moreover, since it consists of a contribution by the persons concerned to the economic development of the country, this compulsory service is also incompatible with Article 1(b) of the Abolition of Forced Labor Convention, 1957 (No. 105), which has also been ratified by Algeria.[83]

In other instances the government concerned has indicated that it no longer applies an obligation to work for national development, but this change has not appeared in national legislation, or the Government concerned has not yet

83 Observation concerning the application of Convention No. 29 by Algeria, adopted 2012, Report of the Committee of Experts on the Application of Conventions and Recommendations, submitted to the International Labor Conference in June 2013.

communicated new texts. See, for instance, the following extract from a Committee of Experts' comment:

> *Compulsory agricultural work.* For many years, the Committee has been requesting the Government to take the necessary measures to bring a number of texts providing for the compulsory participation in certain types of agricultural work into line with the Convention. It has stressed the need to set out in the legislation the voluntary nature of agricultural work resulting from obligations relating to the conservation and utilization of the land and the obligation to recreate and maintain minimum areas of fruit crops (Ordinances Nos. 710/275 and 710/276 of 25 October 1979), as well as the need to formally repeal certain texts on compulsory cultivation, porterage and public works (Decree of 14 July 1952, Ordinance No. 1286 of 10 July 1953 and the Decree of 10 May 1957). ***Noting that the Government previously indicated that these texts, which dated from the colonial period, had been repealed and that the voluntary nature of agricultural work had now been set out in the legislation, the Committee requests the Government once again to send a copy of the texts that repeal the abovementioned legislation and set out the voluntary nature of agricultural work.***[84]

There are also cases in which the obligation does not necessarily arise from legislation, but in which the authorities have failed to take effective action to halt such practices imposed by customary law:

> Articles 1(1) and 2(1) of the Convention. Legislation concerning compulsory public works or services. The Committee previously noted that the Swazi Administration Order No. 6 of 1998 (which provided for the duty of Swazis to obey orders requiring participation in compulsory works, such as e.g. compulsory cultivation, anti-soil erosion works and the making, maintenance and protection of roads, enforceable with severe penalties for non-compliance), had been declared null and void by the High Court of Swaziland (Case No. 2823/2000). The Committee asked the Government to provide information on the practical consequences of this decision.
>
> The Government indicates in its report that the above Order is null and void, and there have been no reported cases of forced labor. It also

84 Observation concerning the application of Convention No. 29 by Burundi, adopted 2012, Report of the Committee of Experts on the Application of Conventions and Recommendations, submitted to the International Labor Conference in June 2013.

states that Swazi citizens and the international community are encouraged to report the incidents of forced labor to the courts.

The Committee notes, however, that in a communication dated 30 August 2011 received from the Swaziland Federation of Trade Unions (SFTU), the SFTU alleges that the High Court's nullification of the Order has never assisted in any manner in halting forced labor practices, which are rooted in the well established and institutionalized customary law through cultural activities which are largely unregulated. According to the allegations, the customary practice of "Kuhlehla" (rendering services to the local Chief or King) is still practiced and enforced with punitive measures for refusal to attend.

The Committee notes that this communication was sent to the Government, on 26 September 2011, for such comments as it may wish to make on the matters raised therein. ***The Committee hopes that the Government will supply such comments in its next report, as well as the information on measures taken or envisaged to ensure the observance of the Convention.***[85]

Workfare. An emerging concept, usually raised by ILO supervision under the social security Conventions but also under the forced labor Conventions, is the concept of workfare. See the following extract from the 2011 General Survey by the Committee of Experts on Social Security:[86]

Negation of compulsory work by the concepts of suitable and freely chosen employment

224. The Committee observes that in the last decade the move towards the active labor market policies was accompanied by the introduction into the legislation of several countries regulating unemployment insurance of the rule, according to which unemployment benefit shall not be paid to persons who without adequate reasons refuse to take up "reasonable employment" offered to them. The overall purpose of the changes has been to "motivate" the unemployed into having the necessary will and readiness to match, at any

85 Observation concerning the application of Convention No. 29 by Swaziland, adopted 2011, Report of the Committee of Experts on the Application of Conventions and Recommendations, submitted to the International Labor Conference in June 2012.

86 General Survey concerning social security instruments in light of the 2008 Declaration on Social Justice for a Fair Globalization, ILO, Committee of Experts on the Application of Conventions and Recommendations, International Labor Conference, 100th Session, 2011.

time, the requirements of the labor market. This "motivation" was achieved, inter alia, by replacing the previously applicable rule by which a person could be disqualified from receiving unemployment benefit for having refused "suitable employment", by the more restrictive concept of withdrawing the benefit for refusing employment offered "without reasonable grounds". The concept of "suitable employment", referred to in Article 20 of Convention No. 102 and defined in Article 21(2) of Convention No. 168, was abandoned to the effect that unemployed persons were placed under the duty to apply for and take up immediately any ordinary work a person is able to perform. Failure to do so implied loss of unemployment benefit for several weeks. Moreover, a person who, without valid reason, refused to take up or left an ordinary job or an offer for activation made by the public employment service, was considered to be self-induced unemployed and was condemned to bear the same sanction.

225. The Committee considered that such legal provisions might have the effect of compelling unemployed persons, under the threat of the withdrawal of entitlement to the benefit, to take up any ordinary job for which they are physically and mentally fit, notwithstanding their professional skills, qualifications, acquired experience and length of service in former occupation—criteria specified by Article 21(2) of Convention No. 168. The Committee observed that "motivation" of unemployed persons subordinating their will and professional aspirations to the dictate of the labor market goes against the very objectives of social security enshrined in the ILO standards based on the concept of "suitable employment". In the context of Article 20(f) of Convention No. 168 referring to the use of the employment services for placing the unemployed person in "suitable employment", the concept of suitable employment fulfils, besides the economic goal of preserving the overall quality of a workforce that takes maximum advantage of available skills and talents, the no less important social goal of preserving workers against compulsion and affront to their human dignity occurring when they are forced to perform work below their level of education and skills. The term "suitable" guarantees, in fact, that any employment offered by the employment service will be considered in respect of its quality, having regard to the qualifications and skills of the individual jobseeker. Similarly, unemployed persons themselves will be treated with due regard for their professional and social status and not as ordinary laborers physically and mentally fit for any job.

While the concept of ensuring that recipients of unemployment benefits are actively seeking gainful employment is not abhorrent in itself, this approach vividly recalls the ILO criticism of the Soviet Union before the fall of the Communist system for requiring unemployed persons to take any job offered them, and the characterization of such an imposition as forced labor.

C Everyone has the Right to . . . . Just and Favourable Conditions of Work . . .

This very broad and non-specific expression was fleshed out in the International Covenant on Economic, Social and Cultural Rights as follows:

Article 7

The States Parties to the present Covenant recognize the right of everyone to the enjoyment of just and favourable conditions of work which ensure, in particular:

(a) Remuneration which provides all workers, as a minimum, with:
  (i) Fair wages and equal remuneration for work of equal value without distinction of any kind, in particular women being guaranteed conditions of work not inferior to those enjoyed by men, with equal pay for equal work;
  (ii) A decent living for themselves and their families in accordance with the provisions of the present Covenant;
(b) Safe and healthy working conditions;
(c) Equal opportunity for everyone to be promoted in his employment to an appropriate higher level, subject to no considerations other than those of seniority and competence;
(d) Rest, leisure and reasonable limitation of working hours and periodic holidays with pay, as well as remuneration for public holidays.

The Additional Protocol to the American Convention on Human Rights in the Area of Economic, Social and Cultural Rights (the 'Protocol of San Salvador'), contains an even more substantial development of this concept in Article 7 on Just, Equitable, and Satisfactory Conditions of Work:

> The States Parties to this Protocol recognize that the right to work to which the foregoing article refers presupposes that everyone shall enjoy that right under just, equitable, and satisfactory conditions, which the States Parties undertake to guarantee in their internal legislation, particularly with respect to:
>
> a. Remuneration which guarantees, as a minimum, to all workers dignified and decent living conditions for them and their families and fair and equal wages for equal work, without distinction;

b. The right of every worker to follow his vocation and to devote himself to the activity that best fulfills his expectations and to change employment in accordance with the pertinent national regulations;
c. The right of every worker to promotion or upward mobility in his employment, for which purpose account shall be taken of his qualifications, competence, integrity and seniority;
d. Stability of employment, subject to the nature of each industry and occupation and the causes for just separation. In cases of unjustified dismissal, the worker shall have the right to indemnity or to reinstatement on the job or any other benefits provided by domestic legislation;
e. Safety and hygiene at work;
f. The prohibition of night work or unhealthy or dangerous working conditions and, in general, of all work which jeopardizes health, safety, or morals, for persons under 18 years of age. As regards minors under the age of 16, the work day shall be subordinated to the provisions regarding compulsory education and in no case shall work constitute an impediment to school attendance or a limitation on benefiting from education received;
g. A reasonable limitation of working hours, both daily and weekly. The days shall be shorter in the case of dangerous or unhealthy work or of night work;
h. Rest, leisure and paid vacations as well as remuneration for national holidays.

There are many aspects of 'just and favourable conditions' that could be considered here, comprising in many ways the entire canon of ILO standards on conditions of work. We will concentrate, however, on subparagraphs (b) and (d) of Article 7 of the Covenant, as the other aspects are examined under other provisions of the UDHR. See the chapters of this volume on equality of opportunity and treatment.

1 *Safe and Healthy Working Conditions*

The importance of this subject is illustrated by the following figures from the ILO:[87]

87 From the ILO web site, consulted 28 April 2013: http://www.ilo.org/global/topics/safety-and-health-at-work/lang--en/index.htm.

Every 15 **seconds, a worker dies** from a work-related accident or disease.

Every 15 **seconds, 160 workers** have a **work-related accident**.

Every day, 6,300 people die as a result of occupational accidents or work-related diseases—more than 2.3 million deaths per year. 317 million accidents occur on the job annually; many of these resulting in extended absences from work.

The human cost of this daily adversity is vast and the economic burden of poor occupational safety and health practices is estimated at 4 per cent of global Gross Domestic Product each year.

The safety and health conditions at work are very different between countries, economic sectors and social groups. Deaths and injuries take a particularly heavy toll in developing countries, where a large part of the population is engaged in hazardous activities, such as agriculture, fishing and mining. Throughout the world, the poorest and least protected—often women, children and migrants—are among the most affected.

a The International Labor Organisation

The ILO has adopted more than forty Conventions and Recommendations specifically dealing with occupational safety and health, as well as over forty codes of practice which, while not having the same status as instruments adopted by the Conference, enjoy considerable prestige and are widely followed at the national level when adopting laws and regulations on occupational safety and health (OSH).[88] In addition, a number of other ILO Conventions and Recommendations deal with some aspect of OSH.

Other organizations, and in particular the International Standards Organization, have issued safety and health standards. These are adopted on a more technical basis than the ILO standards, and the ISO is not an intergovernmental organization, but they are widely followed. ISO standards can lead to a verification process and certification.

ILO standard setting in this area has gone through different phases. From 1919 until 1960 (and on occasion after this date), there was a piecemeal approach, with the adoption of detailed standards of limited scope. These standards focused on a particular danger—a product or a process, such as heavy weights carried by workers, or the use of asbestos or ionising radiation. These standards concentrated on safety and protection from these dangers. Many of them also dealt with particular industries, such as work on planta-

---

88 See the listing of ILO standards and Codes of Practice at http://www.ilo.org/safework/info/standards-and-instruments/lang--en/index.htm.

tions or at sea, and prescribed approaches to mitigate the dangers inherent in working in these occupations.

In the period 1960 to 1970, the focus began to shift towards safety and health protection and prevention, and to adapting the work environment to the workers rather than simply protecting the workers from the dangers they encountered.

A more systematic approach was undertaken beginning with the Occupational Safety and Health Convention (No. 155), adopted in 1981. This Convention focused squarely on prevention and on the adoption of a broad policy approach rather than a mitigation approach. Its Article 4 required ratifying States to "formulate, implement and periodically review a coherent national policy [...] to prevent accidents and injury to health ... by minimizing as far as is reasonably practicable the causes of hazards inherent in the working environment". This Convention has been widely ratified (60 by April 2013), and in 2002 was supplemented by a Protocol requiring the collection of systematic information and notification to the national authorities of accidents and diseases with a view to the compilation of statistics.

The paradigm shifted again with the adoption in 2006 of the Promotional Framework for Occupational Safety and Health Convention (No. 187) which in Article 1(d) refers to "a culture in which the right to a safe and healthy working environment is respected at all levels, where government, employers and workers actively participate in securing a safe and healthy working environment through a system of defined rights, responsibilities and duties, and where the principle of prevention is accorded the highest priority". This reflects directly the approach envisaged by the UDHR and by the ICESCR.

A related question, and necessary for assuring OSH, is labor administration including labor inspection. The law enforcement and advisory aspects of labor inspection are very important to the proper implementation of these rights. There are three principal ILO instruments on labor inspection: the Labor Inspection Convention, 1947 (No. 81) and a Protocol to this Convention adopted in 1995 to extend its scope, and the Labor Inspection (Agriculture) Convention, 1969 (No. 129).

As was stated in a paper submitted to the ILO Governing Body[89] in 2010:

> 4. The current economic crisis has created multiple challenges for national systems of labor administration. The primary challenge has been the rapid increase in responsibilities entrusted to labor ministries and their agencies. The deteriorating economic

89 ILO Governing Body document GB.308/5(Add.) (June 2010).

conditions and resulting social disruption has led a majority of countries to adopt rescue programmes that represent a significant increase in traditional areas of labor policy, such as employment, training, and social security, protection of vulnerable groups and the enforcement of labor laws.

5. Labor administrations are also facing consequences of past decisions. In many cases, the institutional capacity of labor administrations was weakened through reduced staff and financial resources following structural adjustment policies and other austerity measures. The political importance of labor ministries suffered as did their voice in policy debates and their influence on budgetary allocations. As a result, in some countries labor administrations even lost their capacity to deliver traditional services. The growth of the informal economy and the undermining of traditional employment also narrowed the scope of action of labor administration. Moreover, the apparent discrepancy between growing needs and reduced resources is likely to worsen in the near future because of significant fiscal consolidation, which is being carried out today in many parts of the world. As the crisis has reduced the amount of resources available to all state administrations, the prioritization of choices will be of utmost importance.

This is therefore an instance of the world-wide financial crisis that began in 2008 having a marked, albeit indirect, negative effect on the respect for the rights laid down in the Universal Declaration and in ILO and UN standards. This comment applies, of course, also to many other aspects of workers' rights covered in this volume. This is something that needs to be taken into account in evaluating governments' efforts to apply these provisions of the Universal Declaration, even if it cannot be used as an excuse for failing to make all the efforts possible to guarantee these rights. This is, indeed, one of the reasons for the existence of international standards, which is to establish a 'floor' under the rights contained in them, and to help ensure that continuing efforts will be made even when implementation is difficult.

The question of occupational safety and health is also an integral part of other standards adopted both by the ILO and at the regional levels. Among ILO standards, reference may be made to the Indigenous and Tribal Peoples Convention, 1989 (No. 169), which includes a section on working conditions. Article 20 of that Convention includes the following requirements:

2. Governments shall do everything possible to prevent any discrimination between workers belonging to the peoples concerned and other workers, in particular as regards:

...

(c) medical and social assistance, occupational safety and health, all social security benefits and any other occupationally related benefits, and housing;

...

3. The measures taken shall include measures to ensure:

...

(b) that workers belonging to these peoples are not subjected to working conditions hazardous to their health, in particular through exposure to pesticides or other toxic substances;

b International Supervision

The ILO Committee of Experts naturally makes a large number of comments on the application of OSH Conventions, as there are so many of them and because of the large numbers of ratifications. Without detailing them, many of the recent comments note amendments to legislation and policy on occupational safety and health. A significant number of comments take note of gaps or recent improvements in gathering information on problems encountered in safety and health implementation—inspections, violations, fines and penalties, corrective measures, etc.

The supervision does take account of the need for progressive implementation (which is an unstated but nevertheless present aspect of the ILO's supervision, compared to the UN which explicitly embraces the notion of progressive implementation of standards). Here a distinction can be made between different forms of implementing action. It is nearly always possible for governments to adopt the legislation and regulations necessary for respect of these rights, even when the material means of implementing them are not yet acquired or have diminished through financial constraints. It is for this reason that international supervision often concentrates on legislative assurances, though the supervisory bodies often repeat that comprehensive legislation is a necessary but not sufficient condition for implementation in practice.

D Everyone has the Right to .... Protection Against Unemployment

This phrase does not mean that everyone has the right not to be unemployed, but rather that protection should be provided against the *effects* of unemployment—i.e., unemployment insurance in some guise. It is, in fact, a particular aspect of the right to social security that is protected generally under Articles 22 and 25 of the UDHR. This chapter therefore will examine only one aspect of this right protection against the effects of unemployment.

1 *International Labor Organization*

The principal international standards on this question have been adopted by the ILO.[90]

The first generation of standards adopted by the ILO followed the "social insurance" model, which was based on the principles of compulsory affiliation; administration by nonprofit, self-governing institutions; administrative and financial supervision of the State; and association of insured persons to the management of social insurance institutions. From 1919 to 1939 the ILO adopted 15 Conventions and 11 Recommendations, which affirmed, developed and consolidated the social insurance model on the above principles, some of which dealt with protection from unemployment.[91]

The second generation standards correspond to the era of social security. In 1941, the Atlantic Charter expressed the "desire to bring about the fullest collaboration between all nations in the economic field with the object of securing, for all, improved labor standards, economic advancement and social security". Based on the broader mandate and vision established by the Declaration of Philadelphia,[92] the second generation of social security standards established basic principles and a legal framework for the creation and proper functioning of entire social security systems. These standards consolidated different branches into a unified or coordinated social security system, broadened the range of recognized social risks to include new branches of

90 For detailed information on the evolution and content of social security standards generally, which of course includes those on protection against unemployment, see ILO, *General Survey concerning social security instruments in light of the 2008 Declaration on Social Justice for a Fair Globalization*, Report III (1B), International Labor Conference, 100th Session, 2011.

91 Unemployment (Agriculture) Recommendation, 1921 (No. 11), Unemployment Provision Convention, 1934 (No. 44), Unemployment Provision Recommendation, 1934 (No. 44), Unemployment (Young Persons) Recommendation, 1935 (No. 45).

92 Appendix to the ILO Constitution.

family benefit and medical care, extended protection to the self-employed and non-working population. The novelty of these standards resided in the comprehensiveness of coverage in respect of persons and contingencies, as well as in the coherent and codified form of presentation.

The ILO began pulling these contingencies together in its flagship Convention on social security, the Social Security (Minimum Standards) Convention, 1952 (No. 102). It included the right to benefits in the event of unemployment among the range of benefits covered.

In 1988, the ILO Conference adopted the Employment Promotion and Protection against Unemployment Convention (No. 168) and its corresponding Recommendation (No. 176), which consolidated the understanding of social security, including protection against unemployment, as part of a broader set of social policies directed at one priority goal—promotion of full, productive and freely chosen employment. Convention No. 168 triggered the process of more profound social thinking bringing to light the fact that social security was most effective when integrated in a wider framework of socio-economic and human resources development.

However, the standards adopted—evolving, comprehensive and well-thought-out as they may be—have not generated wide coverage and the kind of general protection envisaged. As the 2011 General Survey cited above stated,

> What needs to be clearly stated here, however, is that the current ILO mandate in social security, as reaffirmed and updated by the Declaration on Social Justice for a Fair Globalization of 2008, has largely outgrown the standards with which it has to be implemented. The available means are no more sufficient to meet the new ends. This is particularly evident as regards the objective of extending social security coverage to all, beyond the formal economy to the masses of population living in abject poverty and insecurity, which is placed at the heart of the ILO's mandate and mission.[93]

Most recently, the ILO Conference adopted the Social Protection Floors Recommendation, 2012 (No. 202), which calls for providing people with essential health care and benefits, as well as basic income security constituting national social protection floors. This does include loss of income from unemployment. It explicitly says that people employed in the informal, as well as the formal economy, should also benefit from social security. As such, it should support the growth of formal employment and the reduction of informality.

93 General Survey, 2011, op. cit., para. 30.

This corresponds to a broader adoption in the international system of the concept of Social Protection as being broader than social security, though it flows from the same concerns.

2 *United Nations*

The International Covenant on Economic, Social and Cultural Rights includes the following in Article 9: 'The States Parties to the present Covenant recognize the right of everyone to social security, including social insurance.' This broad statement includes the right to protection against the effects of unemployment.

The Committee on Economic, Social and Cultural Rights adopted its General Comment No. 19 on social security in 2008.[94] It notes in paragraph 16:

> In addition to promoting full, productive and freely chosen employment, States parties must endeavor to provide benefits to cover the loss or lack of earnings due to the inability to obtain or maintain suitable employment. In the case of loss of employment, benefits should be paid for an adequate period of time and at the expiry of the period, the social security system should ensure adequate protection of the unemployed worker, for example through social assistance. The social security system should also cover other workers, including part-time workers, casual workers, seasonal workers, and the self-employed, and those working in atypical forms of work in the informal economy. Benefits should be provided to cover periods of loss of earnings by persons who are requested not to report for work during a public health or other emergency.

3 *Council of Europe*

On the regional level, the 1964 European Code of Social Security and its Protocol, and the 1990 European Code of Social Security (Revised) are the main instruments. Both contain provision for unemployment insurance. The 1964 Code was explicitly based on ILO Convention No. 102 (see above), though the bar was set higher for European purposes. The 1990 revision took account of various developments, including the need to recognize sex equality, and newer ILO social security conventions.

---

94 UN Doc. E/C.12/GC/19, 4 February 2008.

4 *International Supervision*

The ILO in particular makes frequent and detailed comments on the application of the ILO Conventions concerned. For European countries, it interacts closely with the supervisory process of the European Code of Social Security, since the ILO Committee of Experts itself prepares comments on the application of this Code. Many of the comments made refer to the technical difficulty and expense of establishing schemes with full coverage. Since the financial crisis began in 2008, the ILO Committee of Experts has noted in several cases the difficulties involved in maintaining or extending unemployment insurance for the much higher number of persons suffering from unemployment, and in some cases has noted the tightening of requirements for receiving unemployment insurance, with governments citing the costs involved. As unemployment recedes with economic recovery, it will be important to observe whether this kind of restriction remains in place.

Because of the broad impact of social security systems, the ILO Committee of Experts often makes comments of a far-reaching nature, which are intended more to provide a policy direction than to examine the implementation of individual provisions. See, for instance, the following observation to Portugal on Convention No. 102:

> With reference to its observation of 2007, the Committee notes the Government's report received in September 2011 accompanied by observations from the General Confederation of Portuguese Workers (CGTP–IN) and the General Union of Workers (UGT). The Committee also notes the annual reports from Portugal on the application of the European Code of Social Security for the 2008–12 period. According to these sources, even though the minimum standards established by the Convention continue to be applied in the country, recent developments in the national social security system in the context of the economic and financial crisis have featured austerity measures aimed at reducing social expenditure and resulting in greater precarity and poverty. The Committee recalls that the social security system would not fulfil its role if its benefits are incapable of keeping workers above the poverty threshold. ***In view of the fact that poverty reduction is one of the main objectives of the Convention, the Committee requests the Government to send in its next report the most recent and comprehensive statistics on the dynamics of poverty in the country, including data on the number of beneficiaries and the minimum amounts of social benefits in comparison with the poverty threshold. The Government is also requested to demonstrate, on the basis of***

statistics for the period covered by the next report, that the readjustment of benefits for all protected persons has enabled the real value of benefits in relation to the cost of living to be maintained, in accordance with Article 65(10) of the Convention.[95]

The same questions also concern United Nations supervisory bodies. See, for instance, the following extract from the concluding observations of the Committee on Economic, Social and Cultural Rights to one European country:

> 10. The Committee is concerned that the unemployment rate among youth as well as immigrants from developing countries is higher than the national average. It is also concerned that the unemployment benefit period has been reduced from four to two years as of 1 January 2013 (art. 6).[96]

The need to maintain a general oversight function with regard to these broad questions of social policy is important, not only to urge governments to respect the rights which they have engaged themselves to guarantee, but also to provide information to other States on the measures being taken and the difficulties encountered. In this area, it is clear that most nations are finding it impossible to ensure the maintenance of rights in the way they had been envisaged when the respective Conventions were ratified.

---

95 Observation concerning the application of Convention No. 102 by Portugal, adopted 2012, Report of the Committee of Experts on the Application of Conventions and Recommendations, submitted to the International Labor Conference in June 2013.

96 Concluding observations of the Committee on Economic, Social and Cultural Rights on Denmark, Fiftieth session (Concluding observations on the fifth periodic report of Denmark, adopted by the Committee at its fiftieth session (29 April–17 May 2013), E/C.12/DNK/CO/5.

E Everyone, Without any Discrimination, has the Right to Equal Pay for Equal Work

Article 23(2) of the Declaration provides in this form a limited expression of the right to be free from discrimination in one's working life. Although more general statements of the right to be free from discrimination are found in Articles 2 and 7 of the Universal Declaration, and in one limited respect (access to public service) there is a reference to employment in Article 21(2), there is no general provision covering equality of opportunity and treatment in one's working life. This broader question is therefore considered here.

1 *United Nations*

The grounds on which the Universal Declaration intends to prevent discrimination are laid down in its Article 2, and apply to the entire Declaration. That Article provides:

> *Everyone is entitled to all the rights and freedoms set forth in this Declaration, without distinction of any kind, such as race, colour, sex, language, religion, political or other opinion, national or social origin, property, birth or other status. Furthermore, no distinction shall be made on the basis of the political, jurisdictional or international status of the country or territory to which a person belongs, whether it be independent, trust, non-self-governing or under any other limitation of sovereignty.*

Article 23 of the UDHR, examined here, contains no separate indication of the grounds on which discrimination should be prohibited, and thus may be considered to cover the same grounds as listed in Article 2.

The first Convention adopted by the United Nations relating specifically to discrimination was the **International Convention on the Elimination of all Forms of Racial Discrimination** (1965), Art. 5 of which obliges ratifying countries to guarantee the right to equality before the law on the basis of race in the enjoyment of several rights, including:

> e. *Economic, social and cultural rights, in particular:*
>
> i. *the rights to work, to free choice of employment, to just and favourable conditions of work, to protection against unemployment, to equal pay for equal work, to just and favourable remuneration.*

When the **International Covenant on Economic, Social and Cultural Rights** was adopted in 1966, it took a slightly different—and more complicated—

approach. Its Art. 2 provides for the rights enunciated in the Covenant to be exercised without discrimination "as to race, colour, sex, language, religion, political or other opinion, national or social origin, property, birth or other status"—the same grounds listed in Art. 2 of the UDHR. It complicates the issue of "equal work" vs. "equal value" (see below) by appearing to accord the lower standard to women as compared to men. Art. 7 of this Covenant provides for:

> *a.* *remuneration which provides all workers, as a minimum, with:*
> (*i*). *Fair wages and equal remuneration for work of equal value without distinction of any kind, in particular women being guaranteed conditions of work not inferior to those enjoyed by men, with equal pay for equal work . . .*
>
> *c.* *equal opportunity for everyone to be promoted in his employment to an appropriate higher level, subject to no considerations other than those of seniority and competence.*

This is important, as will be seen in relation to the ILO standards considered below, because without the concept of equal value being applied, those who claim the right to equal remuneration may do so only if they are carrying out the same work as others. The concept of equal value, on the other hand, recognizes that different groups—whether it be women, ethnic groups or others—are regularly relegated to certain types of jobs that may be undervalued compared to those normally carried out by more privileged groups. Later UN standards moved on to the concept of equal value, for instance the Convention on the Elimination of All Forms of Discrimination against Women (below), adopted 13 years later.

It may be noted as a general comment that when States have ratified different instruments that do not include exactly the same standards, they should apply the higher standard rather than relying on a lower one. The ILO Constitution indeed provides explicitly for this kind of conflict in art. 19 (8):

> 8. In no case shall the adoption of any Convention or Recommendation by the Conference, or the ratification of any Convention by any Member, be deemed to affect any law, award, custom or agreement which ensures more favourable conditions to the workers concerned than those provided for in the Convention or Recommendation.

This is however a particular problem in the area of discrimination where the fact that equal pay for work of 'equal value' is a higher standard than equal pay for 'equal work' has historically not been evident to a number of governments that ratified the Conventions on the subject. And indeed, the concept of non-discrimination appears to be learned behavior of a kind that often requires social change, as witnessed by the gradual acceptance of the idea that equality between races, sexes, persons of different sexual orientation, etc., is something that takes place progressively. And as it does, the different supervisory bodies read the changing awareness into conventions that were originally intended to be much narrower.

The **International Convention on the Suppression and Punishment of the Crime of *Apartheid*** (1973)—now without practical application—was not focussed on labor as such, though it is of course inherently devoted to prohibiting a particular form of racial discrimination. It does contain provisions applicable to discrimination in the workplace. Its Art. II defines "the crime of *apartheid*" as including the following "inhuman acts":

> (c) *Any legislative measures or other measures calculated to prevent a racial group or groups from participation in the political, social, economic and cultural life of the country . . . in particular by denying to members of a racial group or groups basic human rights and freedoms, including the right to work, the right to form recognized trade unions . . .*
>
> (e) *Exploitation of the labor of the members of a racial group or groups, in particular by submitting them to forced labor.*

The **Convention on the Elimination of All Forms of Discrimination against Women**, adopted in 1979, contains the fullest description of all these UN instruments of the measures to be taken to prevent discrimination in employment and occupation, but of course relates strictly to discrimination against women, within a general context of protection against discrimination. Its Article 11 provides that:

> *States Parties shall take all appropriate action to eliminate discrimination against women in the field of employment in order to ensure, on a basis of equality of men and women, the same rights, in particular: . . .*

and goes on to list at some length action for the rights to work, to the same employment opportunities, free choice of profession and employment and advancement, equal remuneration and treatment for work of equal value (compare to the ICESCR's lower standard on 'equal work'), social security, and health and safety. It also provides for measures to protect women in case of pregnancy—prohibition of dismissal, maternity leave, supporting social services, and protection against dangerous work.

The International Convention on the Protection of the Rights of All Migrant Workers and Members of Their Families (1990) provides in Article 7 for a general right to non-discrimination:

> **Article 7**
> States Parties undertake, in accordance with the international instruments concerning human rights, to respect and to ensure to all migrant workers and members of their families within their territory or subject to their jurisdiction the rights provided for in the present Convention without distinction of any kind such as to sex, race, colour, language, religion or conviction, political or other opinion, national, ethnic or social origin, nationality, age, economic position, property, marital status, birth or other status.

As concerns work, Article 25 provides:

> 1. Migrant workers shall enjoy treatment not less favourable than that which applies to nationals of the State of employment in respect of remuneration and:
>   (a) Other conditions of work, that is to say, overtime, hours of work, weekly rest, holidays with pay, safety, health, termination of the employment relationship and any other conditions of work which, according to national law and practice, are covered by these terms;
>   (b) Other terms of employment, that is to say, minimum age of employment, restriction on home work and any other matters which, according to national law and practice, are considered a term of employment.

It goes on to provide for the right to freedom of association and protection of the right to collective bargaining in Article 26, and to access to social security in Article 27.

The most recently adopted (2006) of the United Nations Conventions relating to discrimination is the **Convention on the Rights of Persons with Disabilities**, which takes a comprehensive approach to prohibiting discrimination against persons with disabilities. For instance, in Art. 2:

> "Discrimination on the basis of disability" means any distinction, exclusion or restriction on the basis of disability which has the purpose or effect of impairing or nullifying the recognition, enjoyment or exercise, on an equal basis with others, of all human rights and fundamental freedoms in the political, economic, social, cultural, civil or any other field. It includes all forms of discrimination, including denial of reasonable accommodation;...

Article 27 provides a broad set of rights in relation to work and employment, beginning with the following:

> 1. States Parties recognize the right of persons with disabilities to work, on an equal basis with others; this includes the right to the opportunity to gain a living by work freely chosen or accepted in a labor market and work environment that is open, inclusive and accessible to persons with disabilities. States Parties shall safeguard and promote the realization of the right to work, including for those who acquire a disability during the course of employment, by taking appropriate steps, including through legislation,...

See also below as concerns indigenous and tribal peoples, which for the sake of coherence is treated together with the ILO standards on the same subject.

2 *International Labor Organization*

a Freedom from Workplace Discrimination Generally

The right to be free from workplace discrimination is found first in the **ILO Constitution**, adopted in 1919, thus predating the Universal Declaration. The original text of the Constitution provided, in the General Principles, "The principle that men and women should receive equal remuneration for work of equal value". When the Constitution was amended in 1946, this principle was included in the Preamble of the new text.[97] The ILO Constitution also provides more generally for non-discrimination in work in the **Declaration of**

97 The relevant provision—in a curious accident—corresponds to the present provision of the Universal Declaration in French but not in English. In English it provides for "equal pay for work of equal value", which goes much further than this provision of the Universal Declaration—but in French it provides more narrowly for "à travail égal, salaire égal", or equal pay for equal work, which is the same as this provision of the Declaration.

Philadelphia, adopted by the International Labor Conference in 1944 to reorient the work of the ILO as World War II drew to an end, and incorporated into the Constitution in 1946. Part II of the Declaration of Philadelphia declares that:

> *Believing that experience has fully demonstrated the truth of the statement in the Constitution of the International Labor Organization that lasting peace can be established only if it is based on social justice, the Conference affirms that—*
>
> (*a*) *all human beings, irrespective of race, creed or sex, have the right to pursue both their material well-being and their spiritual development in conditions of freedom and dignity, of economic security and equal opportunity…*

Shortly after the adoption of the Universal Declaration the ILO adopted one of the first of its post-war human rights Conventions, clarifying the intent to go beyond the Declaration by providing in the **Equal Remuneration Convention, 1951 (No. 100)** for equal remuneration for work of equal value (this time in both English and in French, the two official languages), as between men and women.[98] In 1958, the ILO adopted the **Discrimination (Employment and Occupation) Convention (No. 111)**, which provides generally for protection from workplace discrimination on the basis of "*race, colour, sex, political opinion, religion, national extraction and social origin, which has the effect of nullifying or impairing equality of opportunity or treatment in employment or occupation*" (Art. 1(1)(a)). Article 1(1)(b) allows additional grounds to be specified by ratifying States. The Convention goes on in Art. 5 to provide that "*special measures of protection or assistance provided for in other Conventions or Recommendations adopted by the International Labor Conference shall not be deemed to be discrimination*", and that after consultation with employers' and workers' organizations, "*other special measures designed to meet the particular requirements of persons who, for reasons such as sex, age, disablement, family responsibilities or social or cultural status, are generally recognized to require*

98 After this, the ILO regularly used the expression "equal remuneration for work of equal value" in its standards. There is, however, one set of instruments which used the "equal work" formulation: Conventions Nos. 76, 93 and 109, which are successive versions of a Convention on "Wages, Hours of Work and Manning (Sea)"; in this context there appears to be no inconsistency with the "equal value" expression used in other ILO standards. These instruments have now been overtaken by the Maritime Labor Convention, 2006, which provides for a broader application of the principle of equality.

special protection or assistance, shall not be deemed to be discrimination." This, of course, lays the groundwork for affirmative action programmes.

b Migrant Workers

This completes the list of international conventions adopted specifically on the subject of discrimination, but other conventions also deal with the subject, or incorporate the right to freedom from discrimination at work in their provisions. This is true for migrant workers, concerning which three conventions have been adopted at the universal level. These conventions provide both for prevention of discrimination between migrants, on the usual bases; and then for prevention of discrimination between migrants and nationals. The first of these conventions (among those still in force) is the ILO's Migration for Employment (Revised) Convention, 1949 (No. 97),[99] Article 6 of which provides as follows:

> *1. Each Member for which this Convention is in force undertakes to apply, without discrimination in respect of nationality, race, religion or sex, to immigrants lawfully within its territory treatment no less favourable than that which it applies to its own nationals in respect of the following matters:*
> *(a) in so far as such matters are regulated by law or regulations or are subject to the control of administrative authorities—*
> *(i) remuneration, including family allowances where these form part of remuneration, hours of work, overtime arrangements, holidays with pay, restrictions on home work, minimum age for employment, apprenticeship and training, women's work and the work of young persons;*
> *(ii) membership of trade unions and enjoyment of the benefits of collective bargaining;*
> *(iii) accommodation;*
> *(b) social security....*
> *(c) employment taxes, dues or contributions payable in respect of the person employed; and*
> *(d) legal proceedings relating to the matters referred to in this Convention.*

99 This Convention revised and replaced the earlier ILO Migration for Employment Convention, 1939 (No. 66), Article 6 of which contained similar but less detailed protection against discrimination for migrant workers, providing also that protection of equality could be subjected to conditions of reciprocity.

A later ILO Convention on the same subject, the *Migrant Workers (Supplementary Provisions) Convention, 1975 (No. 143)* also dealt with this subject. In Art. 10 it provides:

> *Each Member for which the Convention is in force undertakes to declare and pursue a national policy designed to promote and to guarantee, by methods appropriate to national conditions and practice, equality of opportunity and treatment in respect of employment and occupation, of social security, of trade union and cultural rights and of individual and collective freedoms for persons who as migrant workers or as members of their families are lawfully within its territory.*

A certain number of other ILO Conventions on various aspects of migration for employment—particularly in the field of social security and equal protection for all migrant workers' benefits in this context—provide for equal treatment irrespective of nationality, or at least for reciprocity between nations in this respect.

As of May 2013 Conventions Nos. 97 and 143 had been ratified by 49 and 23 countries respectively. As already discussed above, the United Nations adopted the **International Convention on the Protection of the Rights of All Migrant Workers and Members of their Families** in 1990, and it has (as of the same date) been ratified by 46 countries. Its provisions against discrimination have been detailed above.

c Indigenous and Tribal Peoples[100]

Another group concerning which provisions have been adopted prohibiting discrimination at work, is indigenous and tribal peoples. There are two international conventions on the subject, both adopted by the ILO with the participation of the rest of the international system in 1957 and 1989 respectively. The **Indigenous and Tribal Populations Convention, 1957 (No. 107)** states in Art. 15 that:

100 Note that the ILO uses the term 'indigenous and tribal peoples', which has a broader coverage than the term 'indigenous peoples' used in most of the UN system and in general parlance. There are many groups covered by these international instruments which are not, strictly speaking, indigenous though they share many of the characteristics of these peoples.

2. *Each Member shall do everything possible to prevent all discrimination between workers belonging to the populations concerned and other workers, in particular as regards—*
   (*a*) *admission to employment, including skilled employment;*
   (*b*) *equal remuneration for work of equal value;*
   (*c*) *medical and social assistance, the prevention of employment injuries, workmen's compensation, industrial hygiene and housing;*
   (*d*) *the right of association and freedom for all lawful trade union activities, and the right to conclude collective agreements with employers or employers' organizations.*

Convention No. 107 was revised[101] by the **Indigenous and Tribal Peoples Convention, 1989 (No. 169)**, which takes the principle even further. It provides, in Article 20:

2. *Governments shall do everything possible to prevent any discrimination between workers belonging to the peoples concerned and other workers, in particular as regards:*
   (*a*) *admission to employment, including skilled employment, as well as measures for promotion and advancement;*
   (*b*) *equal remuneration for work of equal value;*
   (*c*) *medical and social assistance, occupational safety and health all social security benefits and any other occupationally related benefits, and housing;*
   (*d*) *the right of association and freedom for all lawful trade union activities, and the right to conclude collective agreements with employers or employers' organisations.*
3. *The measures taken shall include measures to ensure:*
   (*a*) *that workers belonging to the peoples concerned, including seasonal, casual and migrant workers in agricultural and other employment, as well as those employed by labor contractors, enjoy the protection afforded by national law and practice to*

101 ILO procedures specify that if a Convention is revised formally by a later Convention, the older Convention ceases to be open to ratification when the revising Convention comes into force, and ratification of the revising Convention results in a denunciation of the older one—in effect, a replacement ratification. In application of this procedure, Convention No. 107 still applies to countries that ratified it but have not yet ratified Convention No. 169.

other such workers in the same sectors, and that they are fully informed of their rights under labor legislation and of the means of redress available to them;...

(*d*) *that workers belonging to these peoples enjoy equal opportunities and equal treatment in employment for men and women and protection from sexual harassment.*[102]

In 2007 the United Nations adopted the Declaration on the Rights of Indigenous Peoples. While not a convention, it is acquiring acceptance because of the comprehensive nature of its provisions, and its acceptance by a growing number of States and by many indigenous representatives. Like the ILO standards that preceded it, and on which it is largely based, it is based on the twin concepts of equal treatment and respect for the unique nature of indigenous peoples, together with solid provisions for consultation and participation. Its general non-discrimination provision is in Article 2:

> *Indigenous peoples and individuals are free and equal to all other peoples and individuals and have the right to be free from any kind of discrimination, in the exercise of their rights, in particular that based on their indigenous origin or identity.*

Article 17 on indigenous peoples' rights related to labor, provides in part:

1. *Indigenous individuals and peoples have the right to enjoy fully all rights established under applicable international and domestic labor law.*
2. (*children's rights*)
3. *Indigenous individuals have the right not to be subjected to any discriminatory conditions of labor and, inter alia, employment or salary.*

It may be noted here that indigenous peoples are also subject to all kinds of discrimination prohibited in general international law, based on such factors as sex, national origin, etc. International supervisory bodies often refer to the double discrimination to which indigenous women are subjected, based on both their ethnicity and their sex.

---

102 This is, incidentally, the only explicit protection in positive international law from the extreme form of sexual discrimination known as sexual harassment. The ILO's Domestic Workers Convention, 2011 (No. 189) provides in Art. 5 for protection of domestic workers against all forms of harassment, which was intended to cover this as well.

d Protection against Discrimination in Other ILO Standards

A large number of other ILO standards on various subjects also contain the concept of protection against discrimination in employment, variously worded but consistent on the point of equal treatment. In some cases additional grounds are added—e.g., age, tribe or trade union affiliation (see especially Conventions Nos. 82 and 117 on Social Policy (Basic Aims and Standards)). More specialized Conventions of the ILO on such subjects as freedom of association and collective bargaining (Nos. 98, 135 and 141), forced labor (No. 105), conditions of work on plantations (No. 110), disabled workers (No. 159) and others all carry non-discrimination provisions. The HIV and AIDS Recommendation, 2009 (No. 200) is based on the principle of non-discrimination on the basis of HIV status, and the Domestic Workers Convention (No. 189) and Recommendation (No. 201), 2012, are based on the same principle.

3 *Regional Standards*

On the regional level the European standards are the best developed as regards non-discrimination. The 1950 European **Convention for the Protection of Human Rights and Fundamental Freedoms** contains no article on non-discrimination at work, but it does contain Article 14 which treats the subject generally:

> *The enjoyment of the rights and freedoms set forth in this Convention shall be secured without discrimination on any ground such as sex, race, colour, language, religion, political or other opinion, national or social origin, association with a national minority, property, birth or other status.*

The protection in the Convention was expanded by Protocol No. 12 of 2000, which extended the coverage as follows in Article 1:

> The enjoyment of any right set forth by law shall be secured without discrimination on any ground such as sex, race, colour, language, religion, political or other opinion, national or social origin, association with a national minority, property, birth or other status.

The **European Social Charter**, as revised in 1996, contains no general non-discrimination clause. It does provide in Article 20 for non-discrimination in the workplace on the ground of sex:

> *Article 20—The right to equal opportunities and equal treatment in matters of employment and occupation without discrimination on the grounds of sex*

With a view to ensuring the effective exercise of the right to equal opportunities and equal treatment in matters of employment and occupation without discrimination on the grounds of sex, the Parties undertake to recognise that right and to take appropriate measures to ensure or promote its application in the following fields:

- *a. access to employment, protection against dismissal and occupational reintegration;*
- *b. vocational guidance, training, retraining and rehabilitation;*
- *c. terms of employment and working conditions, including remuneration;*
- *d. career development, including promotion.*

The Organization of American States adopted the **American Convention on Human Rights**, also known as the "Pact of San José, Costa Rica", in 1969. Its Part I, Chapter I, Article 1, paragraph 1 lays down a general "Obligation to respect rights":

The States Parties to this Convention undertake to respect the rights and freedoms recognized herein and to ensure to all persons subject to their jurisdiction the free and full exercize of those rights and freedoms, without any distinction for reasons of race, colour, sex, language, religion, political or other opinion, national or social origin, economic status, birth or any other social condition.

The Convention then goes on to include sections, covered by this general provision, on a wide range of civil and political rights, among which are included freedom from slavery and forced labor, and the right to organize, with a general reference in Part III to economic, social and cultural rights. This gap of explicit protection with relation to work was filled 19 years later, when the **Additional Protocol to the American Convention on Human Rights in the area of Economic, Social and Cultural Rights**—the "Protocol of San Salvador"—was adopted in 1988. The Additional Protocol includes in its Article 3 a general "Obligation of non-discrimination":

The States Parties to this Protocol undertake to guarantee the exercise of the rights set forth herein without discrimination of any kind for reasons related to race, colour, sex, language, religion, political or other opinions, national or social origin, economic status, birth or any other social condition.

The substantive rights contained in the Additional Protocol, too lengthy to reproduce in detail here, include the right to work (Article 6), just, equitable and satisfactory conditions of work (Article 7), trade union rights (Article 8), and the right to social security (Article 9).

Finally, the **African Charter on Human and Peoples' Rights** was adopted in 1981. Article 2 provides:

> *Every individual shall be entitled to the enjoyment of the rights and freedoms recognized and guaranteed in the present Charter without distinction of any kind such as race, ethnic group, colour, sex, language, religion, political or any other opinion, national and social origin, fortune, birth or other status.*

The African Charter is not a labor-rights document. Nevertheless, it does include a prohibition of slavery and the slave trade (Article 5), and the statement in Article 15 that "*Every individual shall have the right to work under equitable and satisfactory conditions, and shall receive equal pay for equal work.*"

The **ASEAN Human Rights Declaration** adopted in 2012, while not a Convention, does include the following language:

> *GENERAL PRINCIPLES*
>
> 1. *All persons are born free and equal in dignity and rights. They are endowed with reason and conscience and should act towards one another in a spirit of humanity.*
> 2. *Every person is entitled to the rights and freedoms set forth herein, without distinction of any kind, such as race, gender, age, language, religion, political or other opinion, national or social origin, economic status, birth, disability or other status.*

The **Arab Charter of Human Rights** (2004) contains the following general non-discrimination provision:

> **Article 3**
>
> a. *Each State Party to the present Charter undertakes to ensure to all individuals within its territory and subject to its jurisdiction the right to enjoy all the rights and freedoms recognized herein, without any distinction on grounds of race, color, sex, language, religion, opinion, thought, national or social origin, property, birth or physical or mental disability.*

As concerns working life, the Arab Charter provides:

Article 34

1. *Every citizen shall have the right to work. The State undertakes to ensure employment for as many employment seekers as possible, while ensuring maximum state production, and the freedom to work and equality of opportunity without discrimination of any kind as to race, colour, sex, language, religion, political opinion, affiliation to a trade union, national or social origin, handicap or other status.*

4 *International Supervision*

The supervision of the right to non-discrimination by various bodies in the international system is very extensive. It can safely be posited that equality and non-discrimination are the core principles not only of the UN human rights instruments, but of the supervisory work carried out by the treaty bodies and other human rights instances. This section will focus on only some of the supervisory material—the regional bodies in particular are not examined.

a United Nations

Mention can be made first of General Comment No. 20 of the Committee on Economic, Social and Cultural Rights, entitled *Non-discrimination in economic, social and cultural rights (art. 2, para. 2, of the International Covenant on Economic, Social and Cultural Rights)*.[103] The first and third paragraphs of the General Comment express the basic understanding of the Committee on the extent and purpose of this right:

1. Discrimination undermines the fulfilment of economic, social and cultural rights for a significant proportion of the world's population. Economic growth has not, in itself, led to sustainable development, and individuals and groups of individuals continue to face socio-economic inequality, often because of entrenched historical and contemporary forms of discrimination....
3. The principles of non-discrimination and equality are recognized throughout the Covenant. The preamble stresses the "equal and inalienable rights of all" and the Covenant expressly recognizes the

103 UN Doc. E/C.12/GC/20, 2 July 2009. Note that the earlier General Comment No. 16 of 2005 on *The equal right of men and women to the enjoyment of all economic, social and cultural rights* (*UN Doc.* E/C.12/2005/4 11 August 2005), covers the question in terms of sex discrimination.

> rights of "everyone" to the various Covenant rights such as, inter alia, the right to work, just and favourable conditions of work, trade union freedoms, social security, an adequate standard of living, health and education and participation in cultural life.

Nearly all the concluding observations of the Committee on Economic, Social and Cultural Rights refer to equal opportunity and treatment in application of the Covenant, in one way or another—equality between men and women, minorities, on the basis of political opinion, etc., sometimes at length, with regard to several different forms of discrimination. The other treaty bodies of the United Nations, particularly those supervising the implementation of instruments focusing directly on discrimination—CERD, CEDAW and MWC in particular—devote a considerable portion of their questions and concluding observations to various forms of discrimination, often with a focus on the world of work.[104]

Among the many examples that could be noted, the Committee on Economic, Social and Cultural Rights often evokes the need for detailed information as to the situation of various groups vulnerable to discrimination, to provide a basis for analysis and action. See, for instance, among the 'Principal subjects of concern and recommendations' addressed to one State:

> 1. **The Committee recommends that the State party ensure that the State Program on Development of Official Statistics in 2013–2017 includes all the data necessary to monitor the enjoyment of economic, social and cultural rights under the Covenant disaggregated by sex, disability, ethnicity, urban and rural area and other relevant criteria.**[105]

The Committee also often evokes—as does the ILO—the need for comprehensive legislation on discrimination in the respect of economic, social and cultural rights. The following comment, addressed to Denmark, illustrates that even developed countries with a well-developed system of respect for human rights need to keep this subject constantly under review—and also points out

104 All the reports and observations of the UN treaty bodies are available on the web site of the UN High Commissioner for Human Rights, at http://www.ohchr.org.

105 Concluding observations of the Committee on Economic, Social and Cultural Rights on Azerbaijan, Fiftieth session (Concluding observations on the third periodic report of Azerbaijan, adopted by the Committee at its fiftieth session (29 April–17 May 2013), UN doc. E/C.12/AZE/CO/3.

the need to review whether legislation has kept pace with evolving social awareness of grounds of discrimination:

> 7. The Committee regrets that the State party has not adopted a comprehensive anti-discrimination legislation yet, but rather relies on different acts affording different levels of protection to different groups of individuals (art. 2).
>
> **The Committee recommends that the State party take steps to adopt comprehensive anti-discrimination legislation, guaranteeing protection for all against discrimination in the enjoyment of economic, social and cultural rights, as stipulated in article 2, paragraph 2, of the Covenant. The Committee recommends that the State party ensure that such legislation also protects against discrimination on the grounds of sexual orientation as well as disability. The Committee draws the State party's attention to its general comment No. 20 (2009) on non-discrimination in economic, social and cultural rights.**[106]

b. International Labor Organization

The ILO supervisory bodies also devote a great deal of attention to equality issues.

First, one should look at the General Surveys carried out by the ILO Committee of Experts. The most recent one carried out on equality issues alone was in 1996.[107] The next time the Committee of Experts considered this subject on a global basis was in a report in 2012—the *General Survey on the Fundamental Conventions in the Light of the ILO Declaration on Social Justice for a Fair Globalization, 2008*.[108] In addition, while not supervisory material as such, the ILO has been publishing Global Reports as part of the follow-up to the adoption of the Declaration on Fundamental Principles and Rights at

---

106 Concluding observations of the Committee on Economic, Social and Cultural Rights on Denmark, Fiftieth session (Concluding observations on the fifth periodic report of Denmark, adopted by the Committee at its fiftieth session (29 April–17 May 2013), E/C.12/DNK/CO/5.

107 Equality in Employment and Occupation, General Survey by the Committee of Experts, International Labor Conference, 83rd Session (1996), at http://www.ilo.org/public/libdoc/ilo/P/09661/09661(1996–83–4B).pdf.

108 May be found at http://www.ilo.org/ilc/ILCSessions/101stSession/reports/reports-submitted/WCMS_174846/lang--en/index.htm.

Work, 1998—as concerns equality the most recent is *Equality at work: The continuing challenge*, published in 2011.[109]

The more extensive supervisory comments of the ILO can be found in its NORMLEX data base.[110] In 2013, for instance, a search found 252 outstanding observations and direct requests on the Discrimination (Employment and Occupation) Convention, 1958 (No. 111) (i.e., comments or questions by the Committee of Experts on which a reply was awaited). There have also been a number of representations and complaints (complaint procedures under the ILO Constitution) alleging violations of this same convention, and on which findings have been made by a tripartite committee or by a Commission of Inquiry. Such comments can also be found in the same place concerning the other ILO Conventions mentioned above. All in all, the ILO supervisory process concerning discrimination is extremely active, and in one way or another affects virtually every member State of the ILO.

It is difficult to single out the most important comments, but the following illustrates the view of the ILO Committee of Experts that comprehensive protection against discrimination is essential to emerging societies as well as to developed ones, and that protection cover the whole range of discrimination:

> In its previous comments, recalling that the prohibition of discrimination in section 9 of the Labor Law is very general, the Committee urged the Government to take the opportunity of the labor law reform process, including in the context of the Decent Work Country Programme, to amend the law to prohibit direct and indirect discrimination covering all the grounds listed in *Article 1(1)(a)* of the Convention, namely race, colour, sex, religion, political opinion, national extraction and social origin, as well as any other grounds determined in consultation with employers' and workers' organizations, in accordance with *Article 1(1)(b)* of the Convention. The Committee recalls that the pillar on economic and social development of the National Action Plan for Women of Afghanistan (NAPWA) 2007–17 contains the strategy to improve women's economic status, and the strategy to increase the quality of education for women; in this context, the NAPWA also aims at reviewing the labor law to meet

109 May be found at http://www.ilo.org/declaration/follow-up/globalreports/lang--en/index.htm.

110 See http://www.ilo.org/dyn/normlex/. Those who wish to pursue this topic, or others covered by ILO standards, may search the comments either by country or by any particular aspect of subjects covered by a Convention—e.g., discrimination on the basis of sex or race.

> international standards. The Committee also recalls that the ILO project "Strengthening Labor Law Governance in Afghanistan" is under way. ***The Committee asks the Government to ensure that in the process of labor law reform, direct and indirect discrimination is expressly defined and prohibited, covering all the grounds listed in Article 1(1)(a) of the Convention, as well as any other grounds determined in consultation with employers' and workers' organizations, in accordance with Article 1(1)(b) of the Convention, covering all aspects of employment and occupation. Please provide information on concrete steps taken in this regard, and specific information on the role of the social partners in the labor law reform process.***[111]

The question of discrimination based on sex is a frequent concern of the ILO supervisory bodies, as in the following extract of a Committee of Experts comment. This illustrates the gap between the development of social awareness and embedding this new awareness in the legal structures:

> The Committee recalls the discussion that took place in the Conference Committee on the Application of Standards in June 2010. In its conclusions, the Conference Committee raised concerns regarding Resolution No. 162 of 25 February 2000, which excludes women from being employed in 456 occupations and 38 branches of industry, and section 253 of the Labor Code, which provides that the employment of women in arduous work and work in harmful or dangerous conditions shall be limited. The Conference Committee urged the Government to take steps to revise section 253 of the Labor Code and Resolution No. 162 to ensure that any limitations on the work that can be undertaken by women are not based on stereotyped perceptions regarding their capacity and role in society and are strictly limited to measures to protect maternity, and asked the Government to take measures to address the legal and practical barriers to women's access to the broadest possible range of sectors and industries, as well as at all levels of responsibility.... It specified that such measures should include strengthening the legal framework, including ensuring that the legal framework addresses direct and indirect discrimination, the burden of proof, provides for effective remedies, and that

111 Observation by the Committee of Experts to Afghanistan on the application of Convention No. 111, published 2012.

> there are mechanisms to promote, analyse and monitor equality of opportunity and treatment.[112]

Another concern frequently addressed relates to discrimination on the basis of political opinion:

> The Committee took note in its previous comments of an observation of the Trade Union Unification Confederation (CUS) reporting that 21,000 public sector workers had been dismissed because they were not members or did not share the ideology of the present Government and that 128 trade unions had ceased to exist. The Committee notes in this connection that according to the Government, the organization has not backed up its assertions with information such as the number of persons dismissed, the state institutions from which they were dismissed or the names of the trade unions disbanded. The Committee observes that these allegations are serious and warrant the Government's full attention.[113]

All these comments and many more, by the UN or the ILO, demonstrate several things. One is that discrimination is an evolving concept, and that the conventions cited here can never be fully applied as awareness changes. Discrimination is deeply embedded in all human societies and cannot be eradicated by mere regulatory action, though this remains an essential step in the process. The final thing to be remembered is that the international bodies can call attention to the need to act, but that it is up to States to assume the responsibility, whatever international law may say.

---

112 Observation by the Committee of Experts to the Russian Federation on the application of Convention No. 111, published 2013.

113 Observation by the Committee of Experts to Nicaragua on the application of Convention No. 111, published 2013.

F Everyone Who Works has the Right to Just and Favourable Remuneration

Article 23(3)
Everyone who works has the right to just and favourable remuneration ensuring for himself and his family an existence worthy of human dignity, and supplemented, if necessary, by other means of social protection.

Generally speaking, the right to just and favourable remuneration has been guaranteed in international law, without effective measures having been taken to define just what that means. Some of its elements have been identified in various instruments, however. It is sometimes subsumed under the question of just and favourable conditions of work, which normally include remuneration. The notion of *minimum* wages has been promulgated by the ILO in particular, but in this respect as well little has been said about the level at which such wages should be paid, or their relation to securing 'an existence worthy of human dignity'. In more recent years, however, the ILO and other international organizations have been pursuing the notion of Decent Work, under which there is clearly a resemblance to the remuneration necessary to ensure an existence worthy of human dignity.

The 'other means of social protection' refers to income substitution measures, which are examined in more detail in another volume of this series as an aspect of social security, but are also referred to below. The parts of the provisions cited below referring to equal wages, or payment of wages without discrimination, are dealt with under the appropriate part of this volume, as concerns discrimination. It may be remarked that the idea of 'just' remuneration obviously refers in part to equal remuneration without discrimination.

1 *United Nations*

The notion of just and favourable remuneration is referred to in several of the UN's core human rights standards.

The *International Covenant on Economic, Social and Cultural Rights* fills out this notion from the Universal Declaration when it provides in Article 7:

> 1. The States Parties to the present Covenant recognize the right of everyone to the enjoyment of just and favourable conditions of work which ensure, in particular:
>   (a) Remuneration which provides all workers, as a minimum, with:

> (i) Fair wages and equal remuneration for work of equal value without distinction of any kind, in particular women being guaranteed conditions of work not inferior to those enjoyed by men, with equal pay for equal work;
> (ii) A decent living for themselves and their families in accordance with the provisions of the present Covenant;....

The *International Convention on the Elimination of All Forms of Racial Discrimination*, adopted the year before the ICESCR, provides in Article 5:

> In compliance with the fundamental obligations laid down in article 2 of this Convention, States Parties undertake to prohibit and to eliminate racial discrimination in all its forms and to guarantee the right of everyone, without distinction as to race, colour, or national or ethnic origin, to equality before the law, notably in the enjoyment of the following rights:
> ...
> (e) Economic, social and cultural rights, in particular:
> (i) The rights to work, to free choice of employment, to just and favourable conditions of work, to protection against unemployment, to equal pay for equal work, to just and favourable remuneration;.....

The *Convention on the Rights of Persons with Disabilities* provides in Article 27 on Work and Employment:

> 1. States Parties recognize the right of persons with disabilities to work, on an equal basis with others;.... States Parties shall safeguard and promote the realization of the right to work, including for those who acquire a disability during the course of employment, by taking appropriate steps, including through legislation, to, inter alia:...
> (b) Protect the rights of persons with disabilities, on an equal basis with others, to just and favourable conditions of work, including equal opportunities and equal remuneration for work of equal value,...

The *Convention on the Elimination of Discrimination against Women* does not refer directly to just and favourable remuneration, but rather to equal treatment between men and women (Article 11). It adds a reference to relevant protection under social security arrangements.

> 1. States Parties shall take all appropriate measures to eliminate discrimination against women in the field of employment in order to ensure, on a basis of equality of men and women, the same rights, in particular:
>
> ...
>
> (d) The right to equal remuneration, including benefits, and to equal treatment in respect of work of equal value, as well as equality of treatment in the evaluation of the quality of work;
>
> (e) The right to social security, particularly in cases of retirement, unemployment, sickness, invalidity and old age and other incapacity to work, as well as the right to paid leave;

No other major human rights Convention of the United Nations includes a reference to just and favourable remuneration.

None of the United Nations instruments elaborates on the concept in a way that would allow a determination to be made at the international level as to a specific, or even an indicative, amount of wages or remuneration that would satisfy this criterion. International supervisory bodies have therefore relied on the idea of a minimum wage to measure the realization of this right, in spite of the fact that it is manifestly inadequate as usually applied.

The minimum wage concept is examined in more detail under the section on the ILO, below.

2 *International Labor Organization*

The ILO Constitution contains a reference to 'the provision of an adequate living wage', as one of the reasons the Organization was established. The concept was developed further with the adoption of Declaration of Philadelphia in 1944 (incorporated into the Constitution in 1946) affirming that:

> The Conference recognizes the solemn obligation of the International Labor Organization to further among the nations of the world programmes which will achieve:
>
> .....
>
> (d) policies in regard to wages and earnings, hours and other conditions of work calculated to ensure a just share of the fruits of progress to all, and a minimum living wage to all employed and in need of such protection;

The ILO has focussed on the concept of minimum wages as a means of attaining these objectives.

The first Convention adopted by the ILO on this principle was the Minimum Wage Fixing Machinery Convention, 1928 (No. 26), which provides in Article 1 that each ratifying State

> ... undertakes to create or maintain machinery whereby minimum rates of wages can be fixed for workers employed in certain of the trades or parts of trades (and in particular in home working trades) in which no arrangements exist for the effective regulation of wages by collective agreement or otherwise and wages are exceptionally low.

Article 2 goes on to provide that

> Each Member ... shall be free to decide, after consultation ... in which trades or parts of trades, and in particular in which home working trades or parts of such trades, the minimum wage-fixing machinery ... shall be applied.

Similar provisions were adopted in respect of agricultural workers in the Minimum Wage Fixing Machinery (Agriculture) Convention, 1951 (No. 99).

As can be seen, however, the notion of just and favourable remuneration, or indeed more broadly of the notion of adequate remuneration, is dealt with hardly at all in these early minimum wages instruments; and in fact the concept even of *minimum* wages is not applicable to everyone and its coverage is reserved to national decision. Some attempt was made to address the level of minimum wages in the Minimum Wage Fixing Convention, 1970 (No. 131), which revised C26. It again stated that ratifying States could decide whether and to whom minimum wages should be applied. It added the following, however, in Article 3, which brought in the factor of determining whether minimum wages were adequate to the needs of workers and their families:

> The elements to be taken into consideration in determining the level of minimum wages shall, so far as possible and appropriate in relation to national practice and conditions, include—
> (a) the needs of workers and their families, taking into account the general level of wages in the country, the cost of living, social security benefits, and the relative living standards of other social groups;

(b) economic factors, including the requirements of economic development, levels of productivity and the desirability of attaining and maintaining a high level of employment.

The concept was elaborated somewhat further in the Minimum Wage Fixing Recommendation, 1970 (No. 135), which was adopted to accompany Convention No. 131. Its first three Paragraphs provide as follows:

1. Minimum wage fixing should constitute one element in a policy designed to overcome poverty and to ensure the satisfaction of the needs of all workers and their families.
2. The fundamental purpose of minimum wage fixing should be to give wage earners necessary social protection as regards minimum permissible levels of wages.
3. In determining the level of minimum wages, account should be taken of the following criteria, amongst others:
   (a) the needs of workers and their families;
   (b) the general level of wages in the country;
   (c) the cost of living and changes therein;
   (d) social security benefits;
   (e) the relative living standards of other social groups;
   (f) economic factors, including the requirements of economic development, levels of productivity and the desirability of attaining and maintaining a high level of employment.

Overall, in keeping with the ILO's general approach in such matters, the provisions of ILO standards address—however sketchily—a pragmatic vision of adequacy rather than the more abstract notion of whether the wages paid are 'just and favourable'.

The concept of the minimum wage appears in a number of other ILO instruments in addition to those focusing specifically on minimum wage fixing.[114]

---

114 These include *Instruments on social policy generally*: Social Policy (Non-Metropolitan Territories) Convention, 1947 (No. 82) and Social Policy (Basic Aims and Standards) Convention, 1962 (No. 117); *Instruments on migrant workers*: Migration for Employment Convention (Revised), 1949 (No. 97) and Protection of Migrant Workers (Underdeveloped Countries) Recommendation, 1955 (No. 100); *Instruments on seafarers and fishers*: Fishermen's Articles of Agreement Convention, 1959 (No. 114), Work in Fishing Convention, 2007 (No. 188), and Seafarers' Wages, Hours of Work and the Manning of Ships Recommendation, 1996 (No. 187), and Maritime Labor Convention, 2006; *Other instru-*

It is only in the case of seafarers that provision has been made actually to set a minimum wage. In the Maritime Labor Convention, 2006, the Guideline adopted along with the Convention specifies:

> *Guideline B2.2.4—Minimum monthly basic pay or wage figure for able seafarers*
>
> *1. The basic pay or wages for a calendar month of service for an able seafarer should be no less than the amount periodically set by the Joint Maritime Commission or another body authorized by the Governing Body of the International Labor Office. Upon a decision of the Governing Body, the Director-General shall notify any revised amount to the Members of the Organization.*

3 *Regional Standards*

The **European Convention on Human Rights** contains no reference to this concept. The **European Social Charter (Revised 1996)** speaks instead of 'fair' remuneration, a notion which may be taken in this context as equivalent to 'just and favourable' remuneration. It provides in Part I:

> The Parties accept as the aim of their policy, to be pursued by all appropriate means both national and international in character, the attainment of conditions in which the following rights and principles may be effectively realised:...
>
> 4 All workers have the right to a fair remuneration sufficient for a decent standard of living for themselves and their families.

It goes on in Article 4 to provide the following, which helps to fill out the procedural as well as the substantive obligations involved:

> Article 4—The right to a fair remuneration
>
> With a view to ensuring the effective exercise of the right to a fair remuneration, the Parties undertake:
>
> 1. to recognise the right of workers to a remuneration such as will give them and their families a decent standard of living;

---

ments: Employment Promotion and Protection against Unemployment Convention, 1988 (No. 168), Domestic Workers Convention, 2011 (No. 189), Labor Administration Recommendation, 1978 (No. 158) and Protection of Workers' Claims (Employer's Insolvency) Recommendation, 1992 (No. 180).

2. to recognise the right of workers to an increased rate of remuneration for overtime work, subject to exceptions in particular cases;
3. to recognise the right of men and women workers to equal pay for work of equal value;
4. to recognise the right of all workers to a reasonable period of notice for termination of employment;
5. to permit deductions from wages only under conditions and to the extent prescribed by national laws or regulations or fixed by collective agreements or arbitration awards.

The exercise of these rights shall be achieved by freely concluded collective agreements, by statutory wage-fixing machinery, or by other means appropriate to national conditions.

In the American region, the **Additional Protocol to the American Convention on Human Rights in the Area of Economic, Social and Cultural Rights** provides in Article 7:

> **Just, Equitable, and Satisfactory Conditions of Work**
> The States Parties to this Protocol recognize that the right to work to which the foregoing article refers presupposes that everyone shall enjoy that right under just, equitable, and satisfactory conditions, which the States Parties undertake to guarantee in their internal legislation, particularly with respect to:
> a. Remuneration which guarantees, as a minimum, to all workers dignified and decent living conditions for them and their families and fair and equal wages for equal work, without distinction;

The **ASEAN Human Rights Declaration**, adopted in November 2012, is not a Convention, but deserves mention as the first international human rights instrument of any kind adopted in the Asian region. It provides in Article 27:

> (1) Every person has the right to work, to the free choice of employment, to enjoy just, decent and favourable conditions of work and to have access to assistance schemes for the unemployed.

The **African Charter** does not refer to this concept.

4 *International Supervision*

a United Nations

More frequent and detailed comments have been made by UN bodies as well as those of other organizations on minimum wages in the light of the financial crisis of recent years. This has resulted in widening income gaps and the failure of many government programmes to keep incomes aligned with rising living costs. One typical example is the following comment made by the Committee on Economic, Social and Cultural Rights:[115]

> 12. The Committee is concerned that the minimum wage, the unemployment benefits and old age benefits set in the State party are not sufficient to meet the living costs and to ensure a decent standard of living to the recipients and their families (arts. 7 and 9).
>
> **The Committee recommends that the State party establish an effective system of indexation and regular adjustment of the minimum wage, unemployment benefits, pensions and other social assistance for older persons, to the cost of living, providing the recipients and their families with a decent standard of living.**

Another example is found in the following question, which it asked Iran in 2012:

> 1. Please clarify whether the latest minimum wage level, as announced by the Supreme Labor Council, has been determined at a level sufficient to provide workers and their families with a decent living.[116]

However, like the ILO examined below, international standards do not go very far in allowing the UN supervisory bodies to say that minimum wages are not adequate, but more simply to ask States whether they think they are.

b International Labor Organization

The ILO supervisory bodies make regular, and sometimes extensive, comments on the application of the minimum wage-fixing Conventions. In recent years the emphasis of these comments has expanded from inquires on how the minimum wage-fixing system works, to examining on a more regular basis the level of the wages set. A striking example is the most recent observation to Portugal on the application of Convention No. 131, following protests from a national trade union organization about the level of wages set. It also demonstrates that there are sometimes differing priorities among international organizations, that may result in diminished respect for rights contained in international

115 Concluding observations on the combined fourth and fifth reports of Bulgaria, adopted by the Committee at its forty-ninth session (12–30 November 2012), UN Doc. E/C.12/BGR/CO/4–5 (11 December 2012), para. 12.

116 UN Doc. E/C.12/IRN/Q/2, 25 May 2012.

instruments. The following are extracts from a much longer comment, and illustrates some of the factors involved in what is usually seen as an economic, and not a rights, question:

> The Committee notes that the Government, faced with the worsening financial situation of the country, requested and obtained financial assistance from the European Union and the IMF, and that... under the terms of the MoU, the Government undertook, in return for the financial aid granted, to only make increases in the minimum wage if the latter were justified by changes that had occurred in economic and labor market terms, and only after the conclusion of an agreement to this end as part of a review of the financial assistance programme. The Committee notes that the Government, as part of the implementation of the MoU, decided to increase the amount of the minimum wage to €485 for 2011—and not to €500, as had been agreed in a tripartite agreement concluded in 2006—and to freeze this amount for 2012.
>
> The Committee is fully aware of the significant economic difficulties currently faced by the Government and notes the conclusions of the economic studies attached to its report describing the negative impact on employment caused by the latest increases in the minimum wage. However, the Committee wishes to recall that "minimum wage fixing should constitute one element in a policy designed to overcome poverty and to ensure the satisfaction of the needs of all workers and their families", as emphasized in the Minimum Wage Fixing Recommendation, 1970 (No. 135), which complements Convention No. 131. It notes from the information sent by the Government in its report that the percentage of full-time workers who are paid the minimum wage increased from 6 per cent in 2007 to 11.3 per cent in 2011, and that decisions taken with regard to the minimum wage therefore have an impact on a large number of workers.
>
> The Committee recalls that *Article 3* of the Convention requires that the elements to be taken into consideration in determining the level of minimum wages must include not only economic factors, such as employment policy objectives, but also the needs of workers and their families, taking into account the general level of wages in the country, the cost of living, social security benefits, and the relative living standards of other social groups. The Committee further recalls that the Global Jobs Pact, adopted by the International Labor Conference in June 2009 in response to the global economic crisis,... suggests that governments should consider options such as minimum wages that can reduce poverty and inequity, increase demand and contribute to economic stability (paragraph 23),

> and asserts that, in order to avoid deflationary wage spirals, minimum wages should be regularly reviewed and adapted (paragraph 12).
>
> The Committee considers that the fixing of fair minimum wages, in concertation with the social partners, constitutes a key element of the Decent Work Agenda and contributes to achieving the objectives of social justice and peace and the prevention of unfair competition, which the ILO has pursued since its creation.[117]

Similar points have been raised with Japan, in the following extract from an observation:

> The Committee notes the comments of the National Confederation of Trade Unions (ZENRoREN), dated 25 September 2011, and the Government's reply concerning the application of the Convention. According to ZENRONEN, the implementation of the minimum wage legislation raises four issues: (i) low level of minimum wage rates;…
>
> Regarding the first point, ZENRoREN considers that, contrary to the requirements of *Article 3* of the Convention and section 9 of the Minimum Wages Act, both of which require that the cost of living be taken into account when setting minimum wage rates, the current rates are fixed at levels insufficient to cover the needs of a worker, and even less so the needs of his or her family. What is more, minimum pay rates are often below the amount paid under the social aid programme (or livelihood assistance). For instance, while the minimum monthly wage is fixed at ¥111,183 in Tokyo and ¥85,679 in Kochi, the amounts paid under the social aid programme are ¥141,680 in Tokyo and ¥112,056 in Kochi respectively.
>
> In its reply, the Government indicates that, in fact, minimum pay rates in nine prefectures were found to be below the social aid allowance but measures were taken to raise the minimum wage in six of them while efforts are now being made for the readjustment of the minimum wage in the remaining three prefectures.[118]

117 Observation by the Committee of Experts on the application of the Minimum Wage Fixing Convention, 1970 (No. 131), by Portugal, adopted 2012, published 102nd ILC session (2013).

118 Observation by the Committee of Experts on the application of the Minimum Wage Fixing Convention, 1970 (No. 131), by Japan, adopted 2012, published 102nd ILC session (2013).

These comments by ILO and UN supervisory bodies illustrate that minimum wages are often set well below a level that corresponds to the living wage contemplated by the Universal Declaration on Human Rights, by the International Covenant on Economic, Social and Cultural Rights, or by the ILO Constitution and standards. They also illustrate that governments often have not used minimum wages to attain a living wage, and that the international financial system often considers wages set a level that would ensure a living wage to be counter-productive to fiscal health. It may be concluded that there is a severe gap on this question between the rights guaranteed in international standards, and the policies adopted by both governments and some international organizations.

In 2014 the ILO Committee of Experts carried out a General Survey on Minimum Wage Systems, which may be found on the ILO web site (http://www.ilo.org). This was adopted too late to be taken into account in the present volume.

G Everyone has the Right to Form and to Join Trade Unions for the Protection of His Interests

This is provided for in Article 23 (4) of the Universal Declaration. The right to organize and bargain collectively is of course one of the fundamental tenets of the ILO, and has been laid down in a number of instruments adopted by that organization. It has also been consecrated in the instruments of other institutions and in international law generally. It is a more specialized manifestation of the right laid down in Article 20 of the Universal Declaration to "the right of freedom of peaceful assembly and association".

As will be seen below, the international law on the subject is consistent between different organizations in most respects, but varies in others. All the international texts agree on the right of workers to join and form organizations for the protection of their interests, usually with it being specified that this should be done without undue government interference. Only the ILO instruments and the European Social Charter extend this right also to employers, and only these two set the exercise of this right in the context of the social function of enabling bargaining on conditions of work and similar questions.

Another point that emerges from both the standards and from their supervision, is that all workers have the right to organize (and bargain collectively, when specified), with different kinds of exceptions appearing for some categories of workers: members of the armed forces and of the police, persons working in the administration of the State, and persons working in what has been termed 'essential services'. The protection and exceptions for these categories, and sometimes the definition of who is covered by these terms, differs among the instruments and on a country-by-country basis. It is also common to these provisions, or to the supervisory processes established for their application, to allow the imposition of restrictions on the actions of these organizations, usually affecting their activities rather than their right to organize as such (though this is not universal). Any restrictions normally must be imposed by law and not simply by administrative decision, and usually those restrictions should be those "necessary in a democratic society" and be necessary for the maintenance of public order and national security, the protection of public health and morals, and the rights and freedoms of others, though the exact wording and contents of this phraseology varies somewhat.

There are variations on all these themes, within a broad range of consistency in all the international law on the subject. The most extensive standards and supervision are those of the International Labor Organization, and the two United Nations human rights Covenants also develop the theme. The European Social Charter has the most extensive provisions at the regional level, followed by the American region, while the African region has no international provisions directly on this subject at all.

At the national level of application, there have been significant changes in many countries in recent years. As the ILO Committee of Experts remarked in a General Survey on Freedom of Association in 1994:

> Over the past decade there has been a spectacular change in the world political climate which has resulted, among other things, in profound changes in the legislation and practice of many States. Although the most striking symbol of these changes was the dismantling of the Berlin Wall in late 1989, together with the trend towards a generalization of a market economy in the countries of Central and Eastern Europe, this evolution was not restricted to Europe alone, many African, Latin American and Asian countries having also opted for, or returned to, political and trade union pluralism.[119]

On the other hand, while the freedom to join and form organizations of one's own choosing has expanded, there are also decreases in the number of workers actually joining unions.

1 *United Nations*

The right to freedom of association is dealt with in both the human rights Covenants, in differing but significant ways which differ from its treatment in the ILO standards examined below.

The *International Covenant on Civil and Political Rights* (CCPR) provides as follows in Article 22:

> 1. Everyone shall have the right to freedom of association with others, including the right to form and join trade unions for the protection of his interests.
> 2. No restrictions may be placed on the exercise of this right other than those which are proscribed by law and which are necessary in a democratic society in the interests of national security or public safety, public order (*ordre public*), the protection of public health or morals or the protection of the rights and freedoms of others. This article shall not prevent the imposition of lawful restrictions on

119 ILO, *Freedom of Association and Collective Bargaining*, Report III (4B), General Survey by the Committee of Experts on the Application of Conventions and Recommendations, International Labor Conference, 81st Session (1994), p. 5.

members of the armed forces and of the police in the exercise of this right.

3. Nothing in this article shall authorize the States Parties to the International Labor Organization Convention of 1948 concerning Freedom of Association and Protection of the Right to Organize to take legislative measures which would prejudice, or apply the law in such a manner as to prejudice the guarantees provided for in that Convention.

There are two significant points of this provision compared with ILO Conventions Nos. 87 and 98, examined *infra*. The first is that paragraph 3 of this Covenant (like the Economic, Social and Cultural Rights Covenant) includes a specific savings clause with regard to ILO Convention No. 87, a provision which may be unique in international human rights treaties.

The second is that the right to freedom of association in the Covenants is limited to workers, and does not take the ILO approach of guaranteeing this right to employers as well. This is closely related to the objectives of the respective instruments: the Covenants both state the purpose simply as "for the protection of his interests", a straight "human rights" construction, while the ILO instruments place the exercise of this right in the context of the social goal of promoting collective bargaining for the regulation of conditions of work and for wider social purposes. This may be linked to the general lack of recognition in UN instruments of this period of a role for civil society in setting national priorities and means of action, a concept on which the United Nations has evolved significantly in recent years.

There is another explanation as well for the exclusion of employers from the UN instruments, rooted in the history of the ILO and of the United Nations, and in the Cold War rivalries of the time. In January 1947, the World Federation of Trade Unions (WFTU), which had increasingly become allied to the "socialist" (i.e., Communist) countries, addressed a letter to the Secretary-General of the United Nations, requesting that the Economic and Social Council (ECOSOC) examine trade union rights. Shortly afterwards, the American Federation of Labor countered with a recommendation to the UN that the problem of trade union rights be referred to the ILO. As Harold Dunning points out,

> Representatives of the socialist countries, led by the USSR, expressed their full support for WFTU and for direct action by ECOSOC.... It was clear that in the view of some members, the ILO could not be trusted to give the workers a fair deal, largely because of the participation of

> representatives of employers. The spokesmen from 'non-socialist countries', on the other hand, declared their full support of the ILO , basing their arguments on the record of ILO achievements since 1919, and the relevant articles of the United Nations Charter and the United Nations/ILO agreement.[120]

The subject was referred to the ILO. In the first discussion in 1947, the Government delegates from two Eastern European states proposed that the word "employers" be deleted from the text so that the Convention would provide only for the rights of workers. However, the proposed deletion was rejected, and the Freedom of Association and Protection of the Right to Organize Convention (No. 87) was adopted with a large majority in 1948. However, the Universal Declaration of Human Rights and the two Covenants based on it omitted references to the right of employers to organize.

The *International Covenant on Economic, Social and Cultural Rights* contains a more detailed treatment of the same subject, in Article 8:

> 1. The States Parties to the present Covenant undertake to ensure:
>   (a) The right of everyone to form trade unions and join the trade union of his choice, subject only to the rules of the organization concerned, for the promotion and protection of his economic and social interests. No restriction may be placed on the exercise of this right other than those prescribed by law and which are necessary in a democratic society in the interests of national security or public order or for the protection of the rights and freedoms of others;
>   (b) The right of trade unions to establish national federations or confederations and the right of the latter to form or join international trade-union organizations;
>   (c) The right of trade unions to function freely subject to no limitations other than those prescribed by law and which are necessary in a democratic society in the interests of national security or public order or for the protection of the rights and freedoms of others;
>   (d) The right to strike, provided that it is exercised in conformity with the laws of a particular country.

120 H. Dunning: "The origins of Convention No. 87 on freedom of association and the right to organize, in *International Labor Review* (Geneva, ILO , 1998), Vol. 137, No. 2, p. 160.

2. This article shall not prevent the imposition of lawful restrictions on the exercise of these rights by members of the armed forces or of the police or of the administration of the State.
3. (Same text as art. 23 (3) of the CCPR).

In comparing this provision and ILO standards, Valticos and von Potobsky point out the relative merits:

> This provision is not as detailed as Convention No. 87. Moreover, the restrictions which it authorizes might reduce considerably the extent of the protection which it affords. This applies to the limitations which, contrary to Convention No. 87, are permitted as regards the members of the administration of the State. This is also the case as regards the limitations 'which are necessary in a democratic society in the interests of national security or public order or for the protection of the rights and freedoms of others', for which there is no equivalent in Convention No. 87. However, the obligations arising from that Convention are expressly reserved by the saving clause contained in Article 8, paragraph 3 of the Covenant. On the other hand, this Article recognises the right to strike, but it leaves the conditions of its exercise to the discretion of national legislations (sic).[121]

Other comparisons come to mind as well, similar to those which may be raised as concerns the ICCPR, in particular the lack of any provision encouraging collective bargaining as a method of fixing conditions of work. In other words, the UN instruments set the conditions for the exercise of a certain class of human rights, but do not explore the uses to which these rights might be put, except that the ESCR Covenant does state that the right to organize should be exercised "for the promotion and protection of his economic and social interests".

2. *International Labor Organization*

When this principle was included in the Universal Declaration in 1948, it was preceded by three extremely important ILO instruments. The first is the 1919 Constitution of the ILO, which in its original version as Part XIII of the Treaty of Versailles proclaimed that the High Contracting Parties considered that the right of association "for all lawful purposes" is of "particular and urgent

121 Valticos and von Potobsky, op. cit., p. 105.

importance", both for workers and employers.[122] The Preamble of the ILO Constitution explicitly cites trade union rights among the measures that could improve working conditions and thus assure peace. When the ILO adopted the Declaration of Philadelphia in 1944, it reaffirmed freedom of association as one of the fundamental principles on which the Organization was based, and characterized it as "essential to sustained progress".

The third of these fundamental texts was the Freedom of Association and Protection of the Right to Organize Convention, 1948 (No. 87), adopted some six months before the Universal Declaration. The ILO was to adopt the Right to Organize and Collective Bargaining Convention (No. 98) in 1949, a few months after the adoption of the UDHR.

The adoption of a specific Convention on this subject in the ILO was not easy. It was put off many times, as being too difficult to agree on, and its lack began to be felt early. When a complaint of violations of freedom of association was received in 1920 from the General Union of Workers of Spain, the Governing Body of the ILO decided it could not consider it without the approval of the Government, in the absence of a Convention on the subject. In 1921, the ILO adopted the Right of Association (Agriculture) Convention (No. 11), which recognized in very general terms that workers in agriculture have the same rights of association as workers in industry—but the ILO had not yet defined the freedom of association rights of those workers. A substantial debate took place in 1927, in an attempt to adopt an instrument on the subject, but it foundered on the problems of reconciling the right to organize and legality as defined by the State, and on the attempts by Italy to incorporate the Fascist notion of bodies created under public law which had legislative powers attributed by the State. There were also attempts to include explicitly the right not to associate, which the workers' delegates could not accept.[123] The subject thus had to be delayed until the more propitious climate created by the end of World War II.

When the time did come, events moved fairly quickly. In the ILO itself, the 1944 Declaration of Philadelphia contained the provision mentioned above. In addition, it referred in Part III(e) to "the effective recognition of the right of collective bargaining, the cooperation of management and labor in the

122 The ILO Constitution no longer includes the "for all lawful purposes" language, following its amendment in 1946, and this concept was also omitted from the ILO Conventions on the subject.

123 See ILO, Report VII, *Freedom of Association and Industrial Relations*, International Labor Conference, 30th Session, 1947, pp. 18 to 21; and Bartolomei, von Potobsky and Swepston, op. cit., pp. 167 to 171.

continuous improvement of productive efficiency, and the collaboration of workers and employers in the preparation and application of social and economic measures" as a solemn obligation of the resuscitated ILO. The Third Conference of American States Members of the ILO adopted in 1946 a resolution on freedom of association which spelled out the basic principles which would be included in Convention No. 87. In 1947, the International Labor Conference adopted the Right of Association (Non-Metropolitan Territories) Convention (No. 84), which refers not only to the right of employers and workers to associate for any legal purpose, but also to collective agreements, consultations and the solution of labor conflicts. This Convention was ratified by only nine countries, and is classified by the Governing Body as having "interim status"—i.e., acceptable for now but probably to be withdrawn at some future time—but it had an important effect on the development of international law on the subject.

Following these developments, Conventions Nos. 87 and 98 were adopted in 1948 and 1949.

Conventions Nos. 87 and 98 are the two principal ILO Conventions on the subject. Convention No. 87 establishes principles and guarantees concerning the right to organize *vis-a-vis* the State, and Convention No. 98 protects workers and their organizations especially from employers. Convention No. 98 also promotes voluntary collective bargaining to determine conditions of employment. The two instruments taken together contain the essential elements for the creation, administration and functioning of employers' and workers' organizations.[124] A certain number of other instruments have been adopted on more specialized aspects of freedom of association.

a Convention No. 87

Article 2 of the Convention reads:

> *Workers and employers, without any distinction whatsoever, shall have the right to establish and, subject only to the rules of the organization concerned, to join organizations of their own choosing without any previous authorization.*

124 There is extensive literature on these subjects. See, *inter alia*, ILO 1994 General Survey, op. cit.; ILO 2012 General Survey op. cit., Bartolomei, von Potobsky and Swepston, op. cit., pp. 165 to 180; and Valticos and von Potobsky, op. cit., pp. 94 *et seq.*

The ILO standards thus go beyond the Universal Declaration in protecting the rights of employers as well as those of workers to organize and to bargain collectively (also provided for in the European Social Charter). As to wider questions of coverage, under Article 9 of the Convention governments may determine the extent to which the Convention applies to members of the armed forces and of the police (note that this is not an exclusion but a permitted limitation), a possibility not found in the Universal Declaration but contained in one form or another in other standards (see below). The Convention thus applies to both wage earners and independent workers, as well as to public employees. ILO supervision has found, in fact, that there is no real limit to its coverage, which extends *inter alia* to the informal economy and even to undocumented migrants. It goes on to provide guarantees as to the independence of these organizations from public authority, including the right to draw up their constitutions and rules, to elect their representatives and to be free from interference by the public authorities.

Several important provisions of Convention No. 87 cover the independence of these organizations. Article 2 provides, as indicated, that they have the right to join and form organizations "without previous authorization", an indispensable right without which these organizations can be made hostage to government priorities. Under Article 3, they "have the right to draw up their constitutions and rules, to elect their representatives in full freedom" and generally to run their own affairs. They may not be dissolved by administrative authority (Art. 4), and have the right to join federations and confederations, and to affiliate with international organizations of workers and employers (Art. 5).

It was mentioned above that the original Constitution of the ILO provided for freedom of association "for all lawful purposes", and that this was one of the points on which the 1927 attempt to adopt a Convention foundered. This provision was dropped in the 1946 revision of the Constitution, but in a very important provision, Article 8 of Convention No. 87 resolves this question by the following language:

1. *In exercising the rights provided for in this Convention workers and employers and their respective organizations, like other persons or organized collectivities, shall respect the law of the land.*
2. *The law of the land shall not be such as to impair, nor shall it be so applied as to impair, the guarantees provided for in this Convention.*

There is extensive ILO jurisprudence on this question, which as will be seen below has concerned other organizations when setting standards in this area.

The fundamental principle articulated by the Committee on Freedom of Association (examined below) is that "A genuinely free and independent trade union movement can only develop where fundamental human rights are fully respected and guaranteed".[125]

The right to strike is not guaranteed textually in any ILO instrument, including Convention No. 87, though it is expressly recognized in instruments adopted by other international organizations (see below). However, although it is not mentioned explicitly in the Convention, the ILO's supervisory bodies have found that "the right to strike is an intrinsic corollary of the right of association protected in Convention No. 87".[126] The employers' representatives in the ILO have challenged the long-standing consensus on this point in recent years, however. Beginning most recently in 2012, they are challenging the finding of the Committee of Experts that the right may be inferred from Convention No. 87, though they are not challenging the same assertions by the tripartite Committee on Freedom of Association. This discussion also involves challenges to the degree to which ILO supervisory bodies may interpret the meaning of Conventions in the course of their supervision.[127]

b Convention No. 98

The most important objective of Convention No. 98 is to encourage systems of collective bargaining. It also provides that "Workers shall enjoy adequate protection against acts of anti-union discrimination" (Art. 1 (1)), and that "Workers' and employers' organizations shall enjoy adequate protection against any acts of interference by each other or each others' agents or members in their establishment, functioning or administration" (Art. 2 (1)). Unlike Convention No. 87, it excludes—more accurately, it explicitly does not cover—one category of workers, "public servants engaged in the administration of the State" (Art. 6). Like Convention No. 87, it allows the exclusion of members of the armed forces and the police, or limitation of their right to benefit from the protection of the Convention.

However, the right to collective bargaining is not as widely recognized in international law outside the ILO as is the right of association. It is only

---

125 ILO, *Digest of Decisions and Principles of the Freedom of Association Committee of the Governing Body of the ILO*, (5th (revised) edition, 2006), para. 33.

126 ILO, 1994 General Survey, op. cit., para. 179.

127 At this writing (September 2013) this discussion looks set to continue for some time. It can be followed in the documents of the ILO Governing Body—see, e.g., ILO Doc. GB.317/INS/4/1, 317th Session, March 2013. See also reports of the Committee of Experts on the Application of Conventions and Recommendations from 2012 and subsequent years.

recognized in Article 6 of both the *European Social Charter* (*1961*) and the *European Social Charter* (*Revised, 1996*). Reference should also be made to Article 7 of the *Inter-American Charter of Social Guarantees* (*1948*), which provides for the existence of collective labor agreements.

c Other ILO Conventions on Freedom of Association

Conventions Nos. 87 and 98 are the basic ILO instruments on this question, but others have been adopted as well. Mention has already been made of Conventions Nos. 11 and 84. In 1971 the ILO adopted the *Workers' Representatives Convention* (*No. 135*) *and Recommendation* (*No. 143*), which provide for the protection of, and the facilities to be provided to, workers' representatives at the undertaking level. Under the Convention, workers' representatives in the undertaking are to enjoy effective protection against acts prejudicial to them, including dismissal, based on their status or activities, as long as they act in conformity with existing laws or collective agreements or other agreed arrangements. The Convention also provides for certain facilities to be provided to allow trade union business to be conducted in the undertaking. In addition, it distinguishes between trade union representatives and elected workers' representatives who do not represent trade unions.

The *Rural Workers' Organizations Convention* (*No. 141*) *and Recommendation* (*No. 149*), *1975*, take a more flexible approach to freedom of association as regards rural workers, and the Convention has been an effective measure to promote rural development in a number of countries. It provides that all rural workers, whether wage earners or independent workers, have the right to establish and join organizations of their own choosing without previous authorization, echoing Convention No. 87. It also provides other protections in line with Convention No. 87, and requires that States encourage actively their establishment and functioning. Convention No. 141 takes account of the fact that trade unions—and indeed national labor legislation—are not effective in many countries in the rural areas, and has been used to encourage rural workers to form organizations compatible with their own needs.

The Labor Relations (*Public Service*) *Convention* (*No. 151*) *and Recommendation* (*No. 159*), *1978* continued the ILO's standard-setting on this question. Recognizing that the right to organize is restricted for public servants in a number of countries, the Convention applies to all persons employed by public authorities "to the extent that more favourable provisions in other international Conventions are not applicable to them". According to Valticos and von Potobsky, "This means that pubic servants who are not engaged in the administration of the State may have a more favourable position under Convention No. 98 as regards collective bargaining, which constitutes a recognized right for such categories of public servants in accordance with that instrument, whereas it is only one of the methods advocated by the present Convention for the participation of public employees in the determination of their terms and conditions of employment."[128]

The Collective Bargaining Convention, 1981 (No. 154), as its title suggests, is devoted to the promotion of collective bargaining in the settlement of disputes and other matters.

d Special ILO Supervisory Mechanisms

All these ILO Conventions are dealt with by the ILO Committee of Experts and the Conference Committee on the Application of Standards, in the same way as other ILO Conventions. In the case of freedom of association and the right to collective bargaining, however, the ILO has made additional provisions. In 1947, as the result of initiatives taken by the Economic and Social Council of the United Nations and on the basis of discussions which were to lead to the adoption of Conventions Nos. 87 and 98, the ILO Conference adopted a resolution by which it invited the Governing Body to examine the possibility of creating a special body for the protection of trade union rights. As a consequence, the Governing Body decided in January 1950 to create the Fact-Finding and Conciliation Commission on Freedom of Association (FFCC),[129] and it submitted to ECOSOC proposals for the establishment of a procedure to put the services of the Commission at the disposal of the United Nations. In November 1951, the Governing Body created a special committee from among its own members to carry out prior examination of the cases submitted to the FFCC; this was the Committee on Freedom of Association.

The FFCC may examine cases only if the Government against which a complaint was filed agrees to the examination.[130] The first governments against which the procedure was invoked refused this consent, and the FFCC was thus blocked from any action until 1964. Because of this blockage, the Committee on Freedom of Association, which required no such agreement, evolved from the original conception of its role as a filtering mechanism for the FFCC, to an independent body which was able to examine complaints, and by now (2013) it has examined nearly 3,000 of them. The Committee is composed of nine titular and nine substitute members, drawn on a tripartite basis from the ILO Governing Body, plus an independent chairperson, and it meets three times a year. Complaints may be submitted by governments or by employers' or

128 Valticos and von Potobsky, op. cit., p. 103.

129 *Proceedings of the International Labor Conference*, 1950, annex XII.

130 Consent is not however required if the State concerned has ratified ILO Conventions on freedom of association, as in this case the complaint could be dealt with under the article 26 complaint procedure.

workers' organizations, alleging that the right of freedom of association has been infringed.[131]

The distinguishing characteristic of the FFCC and the CFA is that they may examine complaints *whether or not the country concerned has ratified any ILO Convention* on the subject—their authority is drawn directly from the Constitution, and complaints may thus be filed against any member State of the ILO. The CFA itself follows up the effect given to complaints if the government concerned has not ratified the relevant ILO Conventions; if it has, the follow-up is referred to the Committee of Experts. This is an excellent example of complementarity among different supervisory bodies in the same organization.

The Committee on Freedom of Association may be the most active human rights complaints mechanism in the international system, and at any one time it has before it more than 100 active cases. After its first few years in which the Fact-Finding and Conciliation Commission did not function, because governments' consent was not given, it has been convened to examine complaints on six occasions. Its most interesting use has been in cases in which another special characteristic of this procedure is used: the FFCC can examine complaints also against States which are not Members of the ILO, if the State agrees, and if the complaint is forwarded by the ECOSOC. Three of the cases have thus been examined concerning non-Member States: Lesotho (1973–1975: Lesotho withdrew from the ILO shortly after the complaint was filed but returned later); the United States as concerns Puerto Rico (1981: the US had briefly withdrawn but returned later that year); and South Africa (1991–1992: South Africa had withdrawn in 1964, and returned in 1994.) It has also been convened for other very important cases such as Chile. In recent years it has been little used, with complaints under article 26 of the Constitution being used to avoid the problem of obtaining consent.

3 *Regional Standards*

a Europe

It is in Europe that protection on the regional level is most thorough, and it is contained in two instruments.

The *European Convention on Human Rights* (1950) is obviously the source of most of the language in the UN Covenants examined above. Article 11 provides:

---

131 See Special procedures for the examination in the International Labor Organization of complaints alleging violations of freedom of association, at http://www.ilo.org/dyn/normlex/en/f?p=1000:62:0::NO:62:P62_LIST_ENTRIE_ID:2565060:NO.

> 1. Everyone has the right to freedom of peaceful assembly and to freedom of association with others, including the right to form and to join trade unions for the protection of his interests.
> 2. No restrictions shall be placed on the exercise of these rights other than such as are prescribed by law and are necessary in a democratic society in the interests of national security or public safety, for the prevention of disorder or crime, for the protection of health or morals or for the protection of the rights and freedoms of others. This article shall not prevent the imposition of lawful restrictions on the exercise of these rights by members of the armed forces, of the police or of the administration of the State.

The *European Social Charter* (1961) takes an approach much more similar to the ILO standards, in its articles 5 and 6:

> Article 5—the right to organize
> With a view to ensuring or promoting the freedom of workers and employers to form local, national or international organizations for the protection of their economic and social interests and to join those organizations, the Contracting Parties undertake that national law shall not be such as to impair, nor shall it be so applied as to impair, this freedom. The extent to which the guarantees provided for in this article shall apply to the police shall be determined by national laws or regulations. The principle governing the application to the members of the armed forces of these guarantees and the extent to which they shall apply to persons in this category shall equally be determined by national laws or regulations.
>
> Article 6—The right to bargain collectively
> With a view to ensuring the effective exercise of the right to bargain collectively, the Contracting Parties undertake:
> 1. to promote joint consultation between workers and employers;
> 2. to promote, where necessary and appropriate, machinery for joint consultations between employers or employers' organizations and workers' organizations, with a view to the regulation of terms and conditions of employment by means of collective agreements;
> 3. to promote the establishment and use of appropriate machinery for conciliation and voluntary arbitration for the settlement of labor disputes;

and recognise:

4. the right of workers and employers to collective action in cases of conflicts of interest, including the right to strike, subject to obligations that might arise out of collective agreements previously entered into.

It will be seen that Article 5 of the Charter deals differently with the right to organize of the police and of the armed forces. The Committee of Independent Experts on the European Social Charter, appointed to supervise the Charter's application, has concluded from this wording that the Charter permits a State to limit in any way and even to suppress entirely the freedom to organize of members of the armed forces. It is only permitted to limit the freedom of the members of the police to organize, but is not justified in depriving them of all the guarantees provided for in the Article.[132] In this respect the Charter has thus gone further than ILO Convention No. 87.

As concerns Article 6, para. 4, this was the first international instrument that expressly authorized the right to strike. This Article was supplemented by the following provision from the Appendix to the Charter:

> *It is understood that each Contracting Party may, in so far as it is concerned, regulate the exercise of the right to strike by law, provided that any further restriction that this might place on the right can be justified under the terms of Article 31.*

Article 31 (1) of the Charter, in turn, provides that:

> *The rights and principles set forth ... and their effective exercise ... shall not be subject to any restrictions or limitations not specified ... except such as are prescribed by law and are necessary in a democratic society for the protection of the rights and freedoms of others or for the protection of public interest, national security, public health, or morals.*

b The Americas

The *American Convention on Human Rights* ('Pact of San José', 1969) provides in its Article 16 as follows:

---

132 Council of Europe, Committee of Independent Experts on the European Social Charter, *Conclusions* I, Strasbourg, 1969–70, p. 31.

1. Everyone has the right to associate freely for ideological, religious, political, economic, labor, social, cultural, sports or other purposes.
2. The exercise of this right shall be subject only to such restrictions established by law as may be necessary in a democratic society, in the interest of national security, public safety or public order, or to protect public health or morals or the rights and freedom of others.
3. The provisions of this article do not bar the imposition of legal restrictions, including even deprivation of the exercise of the right of association, on members of the armed forces and the police.

The *Additional Protocol to the American Convention on Human Rights in the area of Economic, Social and Cultural Rights* ('Protocol of San José', 1988) develops this in Article 8:

1. The States Parties shall ensure:
   (a) the right of workers to organize trade unions and to join the union of their choice for the purpose of protecting and promoting their interests. As an extension of this right, the States Parties shall permit trade unions to establish national federations or confederations, or to affiliate with those that already exist, as well as to form international trade union organizations and to affiliate with that of their choice. The States Parties shall also permit trade unions, federations and confederations to function freely;
   (b) the right to strike.
2. The exercise of the rights set forth above may be subject only to restrictions established by law, provided that such restrictions are characteristic of a democratic society and necessary for safeguarding public order or for protecting public health or morals or the rights and freedoms of others. Members of the armed forces and the police and of other essential public services shall be subject to limitations and restrictions imposed by law.
3. No one may be compelled to belong to a trade union.

This provision is clearly based upon the International Covenant on Economic, Social and Cultural Rights, but contains one provision not found in any of the other standards examined here, in affirming that no one may be compelled to belong to a trade union. This makes trade union security clauses or practices contrary to the Protocol.

c Africa

The African Charter on Human and Peoples' Rights (1981) contains no provision directly on freedom of association for employers or workers. It does contain, at Article 10, a general assertion for everyone of the "right to free association provided that he abides by the law"; and at Article 11 the right to freedom of assembly.

4 *International Supervision*

Supervision of this complex set of rights is extensive in the United Nations and, in particular, the ILO.

a United Nations

The most active and persistent supervision in the UN is by the Committee on Economic, Social and Cultural Rights. In many cases it deals with the right to organize and collective bargaining as one covered jointly by the Covenant and by the ILO standards. See, for instance, the following extract from the concluding observations on Ecuador:

> 19. The Committee is concerned about the presence of restrictions on the exercise of the right to form trade unions as established in article 8 of the Covenant, the International Labor Organization (ILO) Freedom of Association and Protection of the Right to Organise Convention, 1948 (No. 87), and the ILO Right to Organise and Collective Bargaining Convention, 1949 (No. 98). It is particularly disturbed by the fact that nearly 2,000 workers belonging to the Petroecuador union were dismissed and that their trade union rights were not respected.
>
> **The Committee recommends that the State party take steps to ensure that the right to form trade unions is respected. It urges the State party to ensure that trade union rights are upheld and to proscribe any process that would lead to the dismissal of unionized workers.**[133]

The Committee on Economic, Social and Cultural Rights also makes comments based more directly on the provisions of the Covenant itself. The following is a typical example, from the same report as the previous example:

> 15. The Committee is concerned about the restrictions on the right to strike of workers, especially in the air and railway transport sectors.

---

133 Concluding observations of the Committee on Economic, Social and Cultural Rights, Forty-ninth session, (14–30 November 2012), Ecuador, UN doc. E/C.12/ECU/CO/3.

> The Committee is also concerned about the reports received on the practice followed by international companies, in particular national and transnational oil companies, of repressing collective agreements and trade unions and reprimanding of trade union activities (art. 8).
>
> **The Committee recommends that the State party consider amending the Labor Code and the Criminal Code so as to ensure that all workers can exercise their right to strike, in particular those working in the air and railway transport sectors, as well as those in the oil industry. It also requests that the State party submit updated statistics on the number of trade unions per industry, disaggregated by number of workers affiliated, sex, age, nationality, disability, by urban or rural regions in its next periodic report.**[134]

The Human Rights Committee, on the other hand, rarely examines trade union rights in connection with the right to freedom of association, apparently leaving these questions to the Committee on Economic, Social and Cultural Rights or to the ILO. When it does examine the implementation of article 22 of the ICCPR, it more often examines the right of association for NGOs generally, or political parties, than it does workers' organizations. On occasion, however, it raises trade union rights.

b International Labor Organization

Attention has been given above to the methods of supervision practiced by the ILO concerning freedom of association and the right to bargain collectively. In fact, the ILO devotes a great deal of its overall supervisory capacity to this issue. Conventions Nos. 87 and 98 are among the fundamental human rights Conventions on which reports are due more frequently than on others, and trade unions and, to a lesser extent, employers' organizations often use the possibilities afforded by article 23 of the ILO Constitution to comment on alleged violations of this right in reply to government reports. Comments by the Committee of Experts tend to cover most reporting countries each year, and the cases taken before the Conference Committee on the Application of Standards typically include 10 or more freedom of association cases among the 25 national cases examined. When the examinations by the Committee on Freedom of Association are added to this, there is an extensive body of case

---

134 Concluding observations of the Committee on Economic, Social and Cultural Rights, Forty-ninth session, (14–30 November 2012), Azerbaijan, UN doc. E/C.12/AZE/CO/3.

law[135] on every aspect of this set of rights, which is more comprehensive than on any other subject.

The principal sources, in addition to the comments addressed by the Committee of Experts to ratifying States, are the General Surveys dealing with freedom of association (see inter alia the General Surveys of 1994, 2012 and 2013), and the *Digest of Decisions and Principles of the Freedom of Association Committee of the Governing Body of the ILO*, to which reference has been made above. These publications by the ILO both compile the case law of the relevant ILO bodies, and operate as a restatement and development of the less detailed obligations contained in the standards. In this respect they are like the General comments of the UN supervisory bodies, but are much more detailed.

In addition, of course, the Committee of Experts deals with individual cases under Conventions Nos. 87 and 98. In some cases these comments address serious and systematic violations of the right to organize and bargain collectively, particularly when the government concerned does not wish to deal with independent organizations not under its own control. The following extract from a Committee of Experts observation addresses Belarus, and follows up an earlier Commission of Inquiry:

> The Committee notes the comments submitted by the International Trade Union Confederation (ITUC) in a communication dated 31 July 2012 alleging numerous violations of the Convention, including arrest and detention of members of independent trade unions, denial of the right to picket, denial of registration of primary trade unions, and interference by the authorities in trade union activities. The Committee notes with ***concern*** the ITUC's statement that the recommendations of the Commission of Inquiry are still not implemented and that no real effort has been made by the Government to address violations of trade union rights in the country. ***The Committee requests the Government to provide detailed observations on the ITUC's allegations.***
>
> The Committee notes with *regret* that the Government's report contains no new information on the measures taken to implement the 2004 recommendations of the Commission of Inquiry and this Committee's previous requests in respect of the application of the Convention. The Committee also notes the 366th Report of the Committee on Freedom of Association (November 2012) on the measures taken by the Government of the Republic of Belarus to implement the recommendations of the

135 ILO jurists insist that 'case law' is a misnomer, since the ILO bodies have no power to issue rulings. But the accumulated weight of decisions over the years is very significant.

> Commission of Inquiry. It notes, in particular, that the Committee on Freedom of Association expressed its deep concern at the Government's lack of cooperation in providing information on the follow-up given to the Commission of Inquiry recommendations. ***The Committee urges the Government to cooperate fully with the ILO supervisory bodies.***[136]

It will be noted that the Committee of Experts has quoted comments here from the International Trade Union Confederation (ITUC), in application of the principle that workers' and employers' organizations have standing under article 23 of the ILO Constitution to make comments on governments' reports and on their application of Conventions, in a procedure that constitutes participation in supervision and is not a complaint as such.

Other comments by the Committee of Experts are addressed to less repressive States that nevertheless do not fully comply with the Convention, as in the following extract of an observation on Canada:

> Taking duly into account the information provided, the Committee requests the Government to ensure that the Governments of Alberta, Nova Scotia, Ontario and Prince Edward Island take the necessary measures to guarantee that architects, dentists, land surveyors, lawyers, doctors and engineers enjoy the right to establish and join organizations of their own choosing, in accordance with the principles of the Convention. The Committee also requests the Government to indicate in its next report the outcome of the examination undertaken by the Government of the Province Saskatchewan on its labor legislation and its impact in terms of determining the categories of workers which can establish organizations of their own choosing under the terms of the Trade Union Act.[137]

The number of such comments is very high. Shortly before the 2013 Session of the Committee of Experts, the ILO web site listed 180 outstanding observations and direct requests on Convention No. 87 alone—that is, comments on which reports were due within the next 3-year cycle.

---

136 Observation by the Committee of Experts on the application of the Convention No. 87 by Belarus, adopted 2012, published 102nd session of the International Labor Conference (2013).

137 Observation by the Committee of Experts on the application of the Convention No. 87 by Canada, adopted 2012, published 102nd session of the International Labor Conference (2013).

Article 24

Everyone has the right to rest and leisure, including reasonable limitation of working hours and periodic holidays with pay.

The International Covenant on Economic, Social and Cultural Rights elaborated on this in its Article 7:

> The States Parties to the present Covenant recognize the right of everyone to the enjoyment of just and favourable conditions of work which ensure, in particular: ....
>
> (d) Rest, leisure and reasonable limitation of working hours and periodic holidays with pay, as well as remuneration for public holidays.

The right to limited working hours is most extensively regulated by ILO standards, with the exception of European regulations.[138]

1 *International Labor Organization*

As the ILO web site[139] says on the subject of working time:

> The subject of working time has been important to the work of the International Labor Organization since its inception. One of the major challenges in this area remains the need to limit excessive hours of work and provide for adequate periods of rest and recuperation, including weekly rest and paid annual leave, in order to protect workers' health and safety. These concerns have been enshrined for many years in a wide range of international labor standards concerning working time. The process of globalization and the resulting intensification of competition, the associated development in information and communications technologies, and new patterns of consumer demand for goods and services in the '24-hour economy' have had a large impact on production methods and work organization. The end result of these developments is a growing diversification, decentralization and individualization of the hours that

---

138 At this writing (2013) the EU's Working Time Directive (2003/88/EC) is under review. See the European Commission web site section on Employment, Social Affairs & Inclusion, under Working Conditions, at http://ec.europa.eu/social/main.jsp?catId=706&langId=en&intPageId=205. (consulted September 2013)

139 See http://www.ilo.org/global/topics/working-conditions/working-time/lang--en/index.htm. Consulted 6 January 2013.

> people work, as well as an often increasing tension between enterprises' business requirements and workers' needs and preferences regarding their working time. *These various developments are reflected in a variety of flexible working time arrangements that vary from the conventional full-time, "9 to 5" model, such as flexi-time, part-time work, hours averaging, and working time accounts.*

The topic of working time has been the subject of a number of ILO Conventions and Recommendations on two major subtopics: daily and weekly hours of work, and paid vacations.[140] The latest standards on the subject concern part-time work.

a Hours of Work

Until recently, the number of hours one could be expected to work was fixed and predetermined, and reflected the structure contained in the ILO standards and most national law. However, according to the ILO's 2011 report, *Working time in the twenty-first century*,[141] prepared for an ILO Meeting of Experts, fewer workers are now working what has been considered a 'standard' working week in western, industrialized countries. In the twenty-first century, shift patterns and other types of working-time arrangements have become extraordinarily complex in many enterprises. Based on the available empirical evidence, daily hours of work should not be seen in isolation; the entire shift system (or other work schedule) has to be taken into account simultaneously, not one feature at a time. A maximum limit on daily hours of work remains essential to ensure that workers have a minimum amount of daily rest, as well as time for their families and other aspects of their personal lives, but this assurance must be seen in a broader context.

Thus, while the ILO standards retain their validity for many workers, it is increasingly the case that they do not cover all situations.

---

140 All the ILO instruments on working time, except the Part-Time Work Convention, 1995 (No. 175), are classified by the Governing Body (as of 2013) among instruments on which there is 'information requested' or 'to be revised', following the Governing Body's most recent review of all ILO standards. This means that while they are fully in force, the ILO has indicated that they are subject to review in the relatively near future, for the reasons indicated on the ILO web site cited above of changing patterns of work. As stated in the 2011 report cited in the next footnote, the main problem preventing revision is a lack of consensus on what any new standards should provide.

141 ILO Doc. TMEWTA/2011, available on the ILO web site under Conditions of Work.

The Hours of Work (Industry) Convention, 1919 (No. 1)[142] remains the basic instrument on hours of work, though various aspects of this question have subsequently been the subject of 28 ILO Conventions. It applies to persons employed in any "public or private industrial undertaking or in any branch thereof, other than an undertaking in which only members of the same family are employed." The Hours of Work (Commerce and Offices) Convention, 1930 (No. 30)[143] enlarged coverage to all those persons not covered by Convention No. 1, with the exception of those employed in agriculture, maritime or inland navigation, fisheries and domestic service.[144]

The two Conventions limit hours of work to eight a day and 48 a week. Convention No. 1 limits them to 56 hours in cases of 'processes which are required by reason of their nature to be carried on continuously by a succession of shifts.' The two instruments also provide for the possibility of averaging hours of work over a period of time, as well as for permanent and temporary exceptions.

Under both these instruments there is a requirement for consultation with the organizations of employers and workers concerned to fix the maximum of additional hours in each instance, and the rate of pay for overtime shall not be less than one and one-quarter times the regular rate.

The Forty-Hour Week Convention, 1935 (No. 47)—which by mid-2013 had only 15 ratifications—was adopted during the Great Depression of the 1930s. It was an attempt in part to reduce the number of hours of work in order to make more jobs available.[145] As it said in the preamble:

> Considering that unemployment has become so widespread and long continued that there are at the present time many millions of workers throughout the world suffering hardship and privation for which they are not themselves responsible and from which they are justly entitled to be relieved;
>
> Considering that it is desirable that workers should as far as practicable be enabled to share in the benefits of the rapid technical progress which is a characteristic of modern industry;

142 52 ratifications as of September 2013.

143 30 ratifications as of September 2013.

144 Provisions on the hours of work of domestic workers were included in Article 10 of the Domestic Workers Convention, 2011 (No. 189), Article 10. A series of Conventions has been adopted on hours of work for seafarers, which have been overtaken by the Maritime Labor Convention, 2006 which includes provisions on this.

145 See below as concerns work sharing, where the same motivations are present.

The Convention provides in Article 1 that ratifying States declare their approval of the principle of a 40-hour week, applied in such a manner that the standard of living is not reduced in consequence.

In total 16 Conventions[146] and 11 Recommendations[147] have been adopted dealing directly with hours of work issues, but of all these instruments only the Reduction of Hours of Work Recommendation, 1962 (No. 116) is classified by the ILO as being fully up to date, the others having been withdrawn or otherwise classified as out of date or needing further evaluation. Other Conventions and Recommendations do mention this subject among others.

Why have these instruments been relatively little ratified, in spite of the universality of legislation on the subject at the national level? The ILO Committee of Experts has analyzed this more than once. The conclusion generally has included the feeling that the Conventions do not allow for all the exclusions from their coverage that national law often allows on the same subject, as well as fears that States that put into place the protections contemplated in these instruments will be handicapped in international competition—though there is no objective evidence that this might actually happen in practice.

---

146 The Hours of Work (Industry) Convention, 1919 (No. 1); the Hours of Work (Commerce and Offices Convention), 1930 (No. 30); the Hours of Work (Coal Mines) Convention, 1931 (No. 31); the Sheet-Glass Works Convention, 1934 (No. 43); the Hours of Work (Coal Mines) Convention (Revised), 1935 (No. 46); the Forty-Hour Week Convention, 1935 (No. 47); the Reduction of Hours of Work (Glass-Bottle Works) Convention, 1935 (No. 49); the Reduction of Hours of Work (Public Works) Convention, 1936 (No. 51); the Hours of Work and Manning (Sea) Convention, 1936 (No. 57); the Reduction of Hours of Work (Textiles) Convention, 1937 (No. 61); the Hours of Work and Rest Periods (Road Transport) Convention, 1939 (No. 67); the Wages, Hours of Work and Manning (Sea) Convention, 1946 (No. 76); the Wages, Hours of Work and Manning (Sea) Convention (Revised), 1949 (No. 93); the Wages, Hours of Work and Manning (Sea) Convention (Revised), 1958 (No. 109); the Hours of Work and Rest Periods (Road Transport) Convention, 1979 (No. 153); and the Seafarers' Hours of Work and the Manning of Ships Convention, 1996 (No. 180).

147 The Hours of Work (Fishing) Recommendation, 1920 (No. 7); the Hours of Work (Inland Navigation) Recommendation, 1920 (No. 8); the Hours of Work (Hotels, etc.) Recommendation, 1930 (No. 37); the Hours of Work (Theatres, etc.) Recommendation, 1930 (No. 38); the Hours of Work (Hospitals, etc.) Recommendation, 1930 (No. 39); the Hours of Work and Manning (Sea) Recommendation, 1936 (No. 49); the Methods of Regulating Hours (Road Transport) Recommendation, 1939 (No. 65); the Wages, Hours of Work and Manning (Sea) Recommendation, 1958 (No. 109); the Reduction of Hours of Work Recommendation, 1962 (No. 116); the Hours of Work and Rest Periods (Road Transport) Recommendation, 1979 (No. 161); and the Seafarers' Wages, Hours of Work and the Manning of Ships Recommendation, 1996 (No. 187).

b Weekly Rest

It is universally accepted, at least in principle, that workers should have a day off each week. As the ILO's Working Time report (cited in the previous section) stated in 2011, while excessively long weekly hours of work are declining in most developed countries, they remain a major concern in most developing countries and in certain sectors, such as hotels and restaurants, and transportation and storage. Moreover, the preponderance of the available empirical evidence suggests that regularly working more than 48 hours per week appears to be detrimental to the health, safety and well-being of most workers, and that it is important as well for minimizing conflict between work and family life. Long weekly hours are also less productive proportionately than shorter hours and can generate additional occupational safety and health risks and substantial costs for enterprises.

There are three up-to-date ILO instruments on this subject: the Weekly Rest (Industry) Convention, 1921 (No. 14), the Weekly Rest (Commerce and Offices) Convention, 1957 (No. 106), and the Weekly Rest (Commerce and Offices) Recommendation, 1957 (No. 103).

Convention No. 14—with 119 ratifications in mid-2013—provides that the whole of the staff employed in any industrial undertaking, public or private, or in any branch thereof shall, in principle, enjoy in every period of seven days a period of rest comprising at least 24 consecutive hours.

Convention No. 106, with 63 ratifications as of the same date, spanning both developed and developing nations, states that all persons to whom it applies shall, in principle, be entitled to an uninterrupted weekly rest period comprising not less than 24 hours in the course of each period of seven days. The accompanying Recommendation No. 103 suggests that the weekly rest period should be 36 hours, and that young people under 18 should have a longer weekly rest period.

c Holidays with Pay

The ILO has adopted several Conventions and Recommendations on the subject, of which the two most recent are the Holidays with Pay Convention (Revised), 1970 (No. 132), and the Holidays with Pay Recommendation, 1954 (No. 98), both considered by the ILO Governing Body to have 'interim' status.[148]

---

148 The ILO Conference has also adopted the following instruments, now considered to be outdated: the Holidays with Pay Convention (No. 52) and Recommendation (No. 47), 1936; and the Holidays with Pay (Agriculture) Convention (No. 101) and Recommendation (No. 93), 1952.

The main content of Convention No. 132 (36 ratifications in mid-2013) is simple: every person to whom the Convention applies shall be entitled to an annual paid holiday of at least three working weeks for one year of service; and the length of the holiday is to be specified in a declaration appended to the Convention's ratification. A minimum period of service may be required for entitlement to an annual holiday with pay, but it shall not exceed six months.

d Part-time Work

One of the most important trends in hours of work in recent history is the dramatic increase in short or part-time hours. Part-time work is a perfectly viable option for those who have limited time available for work as a result of, for instance, family care responsibilities, studies, or the need for supplementary income in addition to another job. Recourse to part-time work can also, however, be used by employers to ensure that the benefits that come with full-time employment do not vest in all workers. The problem is to ensure protection and a proper balance—an increasingly difficult problem.

Women are over-represented among part-time workers, and their concentration in this kind of work results in significantly worse treatment for women compared to men. Equality of opportunity and treatment for part-time workers in relation to comparable full-time workers is the key issue in this regard. This issue appears to be especially acute for workers with very short hours of work.

In 1994, the ILO adopted the *Part-Time Work Convention (No. 175)*, which had gathered 14 ratifications by mid-2013. Under Article 3 it applies to all part-time workers, though as in many Conventions ratifying States may 'exclude wholly or partly from its scope particular categories of workers or of establishments when its application to them would raise particular problems of a substantial nature.'

Under Article 4, part-time workers should receive the same protection as comparable full-time workers in respect of certain basic rights, covered by the UDHR and by other international labor standards: the right to organize, the right to bargain collectively and the right to act as workers' representatives; occupational safety and health and discrimination in employment and occupation. Article 7 guarantees 'conditions equivalent to those of comparable full-time workers in the fields of: (a) maternity protection; (b) termination of employment; (c) paid annual leave and paid public holidays; and (d) sick leave, though what is termed 'pecuniary entitlements' may be determined in proportion to hours of work or earnings.'

Article 5 requires that measures be 'taken to ensure that part-time workers do not, solely because they work part time, receive a basic wage which, calculated proportionately on an hourly, performance-related, or piece-rate basis, is lower than the basic wage of comparable full-time workers, calculated according to the same method.'

Finally, Article 8 allows part-time workers whose hours of work or earnings are below specified thresholds (which are up to the Government concerned to determine) may be excluded '(a) from the scope of any of the statutory social security schemes referred to in Article 6, except in regard to employment injury benefits; (b) from the scope of any of the measures taken in the fields covered by Article 7, except in regard to maternity protection measures other than those provided under statutory social security schemes. Paragraph 2 of Article 8 states that 'The thresholds referred to in paragraph 1 shall be sufficiently low as not to exclude an unduly large percentage of part-time workers', though no guidance beyond this general statement is provided.

e Time for New Standards?

The 2011 report on working time took note of the difficulties of older standards applying to changing conditions of work. It stated that there is:

> ...an understanding that the instruments in question, although they remain relevant in certain respects, no longer fully reflect modern realities. Nonetheless, there has been a lack of consensus on a possible course of future International Labor Organization (ILO) action on working time.
>
> - International working-time policy needs to find an appropriate, widely acceptable balance between female and male workers' needs (which should include protections with regard to workers' health, safety and their personal/family lives) and the requirements of enterprises, while also considering the needs of the community, including gender equality. In this context, it is understood that there are minimum standards regarding working time that are human rights and should not be subject to economic considerations, such as those which are essential to the protection of workers' health.
> - There are substantial differences in hours of work and, to a lesser extent, work schedules, between women and men. Thus, gender is an important cross-cutting issue with regard to working time, and it has substantial implications for many of the other issues discussed above, such as part-time work.
> - Age is another cross-cutting issue, but the lack of age-disaggregated data is a serious barrier to understanding the hours of work and work schedules of young and older workers.

In spite of these recommendations, the ILO Governing Body—which is responsible for putting items on the agenda of the International Labor Conference—is not currently considering any standard setting on hours of working and broader issues of working time.

f Work-sharing as a Job-preservation Strategy

According to the ILO, working-time adjustments offer an important strategy for limiting or avoiding job losses and supporting companies in retaining their workforce in economic downturns. One important tool for adjusting working hours to changes in demand is work-sharing. Work-sharing is a reduction of working time that is intended to spread a reduced volume of work over the same (or similar) number of workers in order to avoid lay-offs; alternatively, it can be a measure intended to create new employment.

2 *European Standards*

Under the EU's Working Time Directive (2003/88/EC), each Member State must ensure that every worker is entitled to:

- a limit to weekly working time, which must not exceed 48 hours on average, including any overtime
- a minimum daily rest period, of 11 consecutive hours in every 24
- a rest break during working time, if the worker is on duty for longer than six hours
- a minimum weekly rest period of 24 uninterrupted hours for each seven-day period, which is added to the 11 hours' daily rest
- paid annual leave, of at least four weeks per year
- extra protection in the case of night work (for example, average working hours must not exceed 8 hours per 24-hour period; night workers must not perform heavy or dangerous work for longer than 8 hours in any 24-hour period; there should be a right to free health assessments and in certain situations, to transfer to day work).

The Directive also sets out special rules for working time in a small range of sectors: doctors in training, offshore workers, sea fishing workers, and workers in urban passenger transport. There are separate directives on working time for certain workers in specific transport sectors.

The European Commission is currently (mid-2013) reviewing Directive 2003/88/EC, by means of a two-stage consultation of the social partners at EU level and a detailed impact assessment. In December 2010, the Commission adopted a second-stage consultation paper asking workers' and employers' representatives for their views on possible changes to the Directive. The Commission also adopted a report on how the current working time rules are being implemented in the Member States and made available an independent study on the social and economic impact of the Directive.

It may be concluded from the above discussion that, while there has generally been agreement among nations that there should be limitations on working hours and weekly rest, the consensus that has reigned for many years on what those limitations should be has weakened in recent years. The low number of ratifications of existing ILO standards, and the fact that the ILO Governing Body has classified so many of these standards as being out of date, suggests that there is a need for serious reflection on how the provisions of article 24 of the Universal Declaration should be applied.

CHAPTER 3

Concluding Remarks

This examination of the measures taken at the international level to apply the work-related provisions of the Universal Declaration of Human Rights, shows that a great deal has been done, but that much remains to do.

First, there is no subject covered in these articles of the UDHR which has not been the subject of international standards, adopted either before or after the adoption of the UDHR in 1948. The need for a well-regulated economic life—perhaps more important to those who have framed them than a perceived need to protect human rights—has fostered the adoption of many standards in various international bodies, on both the universal and regional levels.

It can also be said that these standards cover both areas which everyone would recognize as encompassing human rights, and the more technical aspects of these questions which are the contributing factors for the realization of human rights. Freedom from forced labor and from discrimination, as well as the right to organize to protect one's interests, are easily recognizable as universal human rights. The rights to protection against exploitation in other areas—e.g., occupational safety and health, working hours, and setting the conditions under which jobs are made available for everyone—fall into the category of being the building blocks for the realization of human dignity at work and respect for workers' rights. Still others, such as those on employment policy and social security, seek to guide social policy in ways that are less susceptible of action to implement them.

Some of these standards have been very widely ratified, but others have not. Those standards referred to above that were adopted by the United Nations—the core human rights standards of the international system—have for the most part been very widely ratified. The same can be said of the ILO standards that express core principles or form the baseline for economic development and progress. The core standards adopted at the regional levels have also known success.

Some of them, however, have not made it off the page of the collections of Conventions. One of the major failures of international human rights law in the economic and social field is the standards on *migrant workers*. At a time when economic integration is growing and borders are losing their traditional power of defining national characters, nations have met often to define the rules for migration for work. Yet though nearly all these policy makers agree on

 | DOI 10.1163/9789004244559_007

what those rules should be, few are willing to commit to their application in their own countries. This is happening in spite of the fact that the developed economies of the West, and some others, are encountering aging populations and will be unable to pay their retired workers the benefits to which they are entitled if they do not accept an influx of younger and poorer immigrants to do the jobs they no longer want to do, and to pay the employment taxes that will fund their social security funds.

International standards on *conditions of work*—the standards adopted to apply many of the requirements of articles 23 and 24 of the Universal Declaration—have met with a more varied response. The international standards on safety and health are widely ratified and nearly every country aspires to their implementation. These standards have measurable benefits and the basic common sense of protecting people at work is clear to everyone. Those that seek to regulate hours of work and forms of employment, on the other hand, are being challenged in developed countries as the nature of the economy changes in an emerging post-industrial society. There are aspects of these subjects, conceived as rights of working people, that are now being rethought and reimagined as the nature of the world of work changes.

And there are new challenges even for some of the basic human rights dealt with in these articles of the Universal Declaration. The right to organize and bargain collectively remains relatively healthy and well-protected by law in most developed countries, though world-wide it is challenged by the huge informal economy in which the legal structures and protections necessary for it to function do not operate. And the changes from an agricultural to an industrial economy that sparked organization of workers at several historical turning points during the 20th century, are less a part of the economic and social landscape of the 21st century, so that trade unions are struggling to redefine their very reason for existence in many countries.

By contrast, the fundamental right of freedom from forced labor remains high on the list of priorities, and indeed faces new manifestations that make it even more vital. Trafficking for labor and sexual exploitation has grown exponentially with the weakening of borders and the ready availability of travel, combined with global information networks that allow many to catch glimpses of the lives they are not able to live at home. The daily influx of desperate migrants to Europe, and ease of entry across borders in North America, are but two of the openings for exploiters of human misery who capture the hopes of the poor and subject them to forced labor. Traditional slavery has diminished in most of the world. But this new slavery leaves us facing some 21 million people in forced labor around the world today, according to the ILO.

Discrimination often feels like the perpetual curse of the human beast. It is tackled in legislation and through growing awareness, but then new lessons are learned about the ways in which irrational prejudice affects the ways we think about each other. The integration of women in the workforce in most parts of the world over the last century is thrown into sharp relief by awareness of the continuing exploitation and subjugation of women for social and religious reasons. And even when equality of the sexes is well on its way to being accepted (if not really practiced yet) in many countries, the newer concept of sexual orientation requires us to think again about the meaning of sex discrimination. Discrimination on the basis of race is another concept that is pretty well understood today, but new ways are discovered in which racial discrimination is practiced in the political arena and in such matters as uneven sentencing for similar offenses.

The one area of the world of work where there have been solid, if uneven, advances in human rights is child labor. This is barely touched upon in the present volume as it is not addressed directly in Articles 23 and 24 of the Universal Declaration. This highlights the fact that it was barely a subject for human rights discussion until the adoption of the UN Convention on the Rights of the Child in 1989, and the ILO's Worst Forms of Child Labor Convention (No. 182) in 1999. But concentrated attention in the international human rights and development communities, together with heroic efforts at the national level in many countries, have resulted in a global reduction in child labor of more than one-third since the beginning of the 1990s. This shows that when the will of the international community is allied with the necessary resources, and with the requisite political will at the national level, these intractable problems of human rights can be faced and overcome.

Bibliography

ILO Sources (all available on the ILO web site at http://www.ilo.org)

ILO Constitution

ILO Conventions and Recommendations (1919—date)

Reports of the ILO Committee of Experts on the Application of Conventions and Recommendations

Reports of the Conference Committee on the Application of Standards

General Surveys carried out by the Committee of Experts

Freedom of association—Digest of decisions and principles of the Freedom of Association Committee of the Governing Body of the ILO. Fifth (revised) edition, 2006

Reports of Committees established to examine representations (art. 24)

Reports of Commissions of Inquiry and Complaints (art. 26)

Special procedures for the examination in the International Labor Organization of complaints alleging violations of freedom of association Standing Orders of the International Labor Conference

2008 Declaration on social justice for a fair globalization

1998 Declaration on Fundamental Principles and Rights at Work

Tripartite Declaration of Principles concerning Multinational Enterprises and Social Policy

Handbook of procedures relating to international labor Conventions and Recommendations (Rev. 2012)

Guide to international labor standards (2008)

Rules of the Game: a brief introduction to International Labor Standards (Revised edition 2009)

Other Writings

Les normes internationales du travail: un patrimoine pour l'avenir. Mélanges en l'honneur de Nicolas Valticos, 2004 (articles in both English and French).

Rodgers, Lee, Swepston and van Daele, *The ILO and the Quest for Social Justice*, 1919–2009, ILO 2009.

Swepston and Tapiola, 'The ILO and the Impact of Labor Standards: Working on the Ground after an ILO Commission of Inquiry', **Stanford Law and Policy Review**, Vol. 21, Issue 3 (2010).

Swepston, *International Labor Law*, in **Comparative Labor Law and Industrial Relations in Industrialized Market Economies**, Xth revised edition, ed. Blanpain (Wolters Kluwer, 2010). (Also earlier editions.)

———, *The International Labor Organization and Human Rights*, in **International Protection of Human Rights: A Textbook**, ed. Krause and Scheinen, Institute for Human Rights (Abo Akademi, Finland, 2009, revised 2012).

Human Rights, Labor Rights and International Trade, Compa and Diamond ed. (University of Pennsylvania Press, 1996).

Vienna Declaration and Programme of Action, *adopted by the World Conference on Human Rights in Vienna on 25 June 1993*.

International Trade Union Confederation (ITUC), *Labor Standards in World Bank Group Lending: Lessons Learned and Next Steps*, 2011.

Mayer, Jean, "The concept of the right to work in international standards and the legislation of ILO member States", *International Labor Review*, Vol. 124, No. 2, March–April 1985.

The cost of coercion. Report of the Director-General, Global Report under the follow-up to the ILO Declaration on Fundamental Principles and Rights at Work, International Labor Conference, 98th Session 2009, Report I(B).

General Survey concerning social security instruments in light of the 2008 Declaration on Social Justice for a Fair Globalization, ILO, Committee of Experts on the Application of Conventions and Recommendations, International Labor Conference, 100th Session, 2011.

Equality in Employment and Occupation, Report III (4B), General Survey by the Committee of Experts on the Application of Conventions and Recommendations, International Labor Conference, 83rd Session (1996).

ILO, *Freedom of Association and Collective Bargaining*, Report III (4B), General Survey by the Committee of Experts on the Application of Conventions and Recommendations, International Labor Conference, 81st Session (1994).

Index

www.ingramcontent.com/pod-product-compliance
Lightning Source LLC
LaVergne TN
LVHW010657300926
849161LV00005B/1155